14.95
12/1/04

# R

# CHECKING
# FOR
# EVERYONE

DATE DUE

# REFERENCE CHECKING FOR EVERYONE

## What You Need to Know to Protect Yourself, Your Business, and Your Family

## PAUL WILLIAM BARADA

With
J. Michael McLaughlin

McGraw-Hill

NEW YORK   CHICAGO   SAN FRANCISCO   LISBON   LONDON
MADRID   MEXICO CITY   MILAN   NEW DELHI   SAN JUAN   SEOUL
SINGAPORE   SYDNEY   TORONTO

1 2 3 4 5 6 7 8 9 10  DOC/DOC   0 9 8 7 6 5 4

ISBN 0-07-142367-2

Product or brand names used in this book may be trade names or trademarks. Where we believe that there may be proprietary claims to such trade names or trademarks, the name has been used with an initial capital or it has been capitalized in the style used by the name claimant. Regardless of the capitalization used, all such names have been used in an editorial manner without any intent to convey endorsement of or other affiliation with the name claimant. Neither the author nor the publisher intends to express any judgment as to the validity or legal status of any such proprietary claims.

McGraw-Hill books are available at special quantity discounts to use as premiums and sales promotions, or for use in corporate training programs. For more information, please write to the Director of Special Sales, McGraw-Hill Professional, Two Penn Plaza, New York, NY 10121-2298. Or contact your local bookstore.

 This book is printed on recycled, acid-free paper containing a minimum of 50% recycled, de-inked fiber.

**Library of Congress Cataloging-in-Publication Data.**

Barada, Paul William.
    Reference checking for everyone : what you need to know to protect yourself, your
    business, and your family / by Paul William Barada with J. Michael McLaughlin.
        p.    cm.
    ISBN 0-07-142367-2 (alk. paper)
    1. Employment references.   I. McLaughlin, J. Michael.   II. Title.
HF5549.5.R45B37   2003
658.3'112—dc22

                                                            2003021605

*For Connie and our sons, Paul Jr., Will, and Jon*

# CONTENTS

# ACKNOWLEDGMENTS

Over the years, I have been very fortunate to be surrounded by some very good people. When I formed Barada Associates in1982 in my hometown of Rushville, Indiana, my goal was to prove it was possible to create an exciting new business in a small town. When I decided that business would be centered around the relatively undeveloped concept of professional reference checking, I learned we could offer a higher level of service here than any of our competitors. This successfully opened the door to a nationwide market that, in turn, raised the bar for quality reference checking everywhere.

Several people with whom I have worked over the years deserve special thanks. Their talents, energy, insight, and inspiration proved invaluable in the preparation of this book. They include current staffers Mardella Huskins, Beth Jarman, Tracy Weitzel, Michelle Heimsoth, and Gilda Caviness. My gratitude is also extended to former staffers Tricia Stamm and Judy Frost. Others who have offered advice and support include Rick Levi, lifelong friend and attorney, Phil Caviness, attorney, and business partners Dick Fleming and Bob Piers. Had it not been for Dick's and Bob's faith in me and our shared belief that a new kind of reference-checking business was viable, none of our success would have been realized.

I would be terribly remiss if I didn't also extend my deepest appreciation to Michael A. Blickman, an attorney with the Ice Miller firm in Indianapolis. Michael is the author of the groundbreaking employer release in this book. He represents employers in all aspects of labor relations and employment matters in both the public and private sectors. He has also lectured extensively and presented seminars on a wide variety of employment law subjects. His assistance and advice in the creation of this book has been invaluable.

One final word of thanks to my editor at McGraw-Hill, Donya Dickerson. She was a gentle taskmaster, guide, and friend throughout the entire process. Although she was not the first to suggest I share my thoughts in a book about how reference checking should be done, she was precisely the right person at the right time to help me make this dream a reality.

Paul W. Barada
Rushville, Indiana

# INTRODUCTION

Why should business managers and human resource (HR) professionals in industries and business of all kinds read a book about reference checking? It's because today more than ever, the difference between success and failure, profit and loss, peace of mind, and constant worry depend on minimizing the *unknowns* in the workplace. Understanding how to eliminate some of the risk factors in business is vital to more of us than you might imagine. Not only do personnel directors need to know if a job applicant is who he or she claims to be, but also whether or not the job applicant can actually do the work. And this kind of business "insurance" isn't only desirable in the executive suite or on the assembly line; it's good to have when hiring a contractor, a food server, an accountant, a nanny, an in-home caregiver, or even a medical professional. References are also key for landlords considering new tenants.

Clearly, making so-called hiring mistakes is financially costly, an inefficient waste of valuable time, and potentially dangerous, whether you're a Fortune 500 company or an individual. In fact, the goodwill you or your company have developed in the marketplace over many years can be seriously damaged—even wiped out—if the wrong person gets hired.

When all the books on the theory and practice of business have been read, when the collective wisdom of all the business schools has been absorbed, what is the primary reason any business succeeds? Is it because of its products? Most people seem to think so. But how do we create new and better products? Is it through a particular manufacturing process? Is it through technological savvy? Is it through the utilization of the most modern plants and high-tech equipment? Not really. Ultimately, it is through *people* that businesses succeed and thrive.

Theodore Roosevelt once said, "The best executive is the one who has sense enough to pick good [people] to do what he wants done, and self-restraint enough to keep from meddling with them while they do it."

In order for a business to survive and thrive, its most fundamental and important function is the careful selection of the best people for the jobs that need doing. This book will help executives choose those good people more effectively.

## WHY REFERENCE CHECKING HAS BEEN SEEN AS PROBLEMATIC

In my 20 years' experience at checking references, it is my personal view that employee selection is more problematic and confusing than any other field of business endeavor. In fact, managers can't even agree on the terms being used in reference checking, let alone how best to carry out the exercise.

This is also a book that combines two seemingly incompatible notions: common business sense and the law—the practical side of reference checking and the legal side. It also contains ground-breaking new information for employers to know when asked to provide information about former employees.

Part of the problem, of course, is that corporate attorneys have successfully intimidated most HR people to the extent that many are afraid to say "'boo' to a goose" when it comes to checking the references of their candidates for employment. And they're just as reluctant to provide reference information on former employees.

Not long ago, I was theorizing with a lawyer friend of mine about that very problem. I asked him, "If you were representing me and I asked for your professional opinion on whether or not I would run any legal risks by getting out of bed in the morning, could you assure me that I would not?"

My friend cleared his throat, sputtered a little, laughed, and said, "Well, strictly speaking, no. I couldn't honestly advise you that there are no risks whatsoever associated with getting out of bed."

But we all know that, most mornings, we *do* risk it and we *do* get out of bed. So, this is also a book about risks. It objectively compares the perceived risks of checking and providing references with the risks of *not* checking—and of maintaining a no-comment policy about former employees. The latter, in my view, is a lot like choosing to never get out of bed—and just about as productive for everyone's business.

## WHAT YOU'LL FIND IN THIS BOOK

A few years ago, my company received a call from a major manufacturing firm in Ohio. They wanted us to do a reference report on a candidate they were considering for a plant manager's position. They said they had already interviewed a top candidate and that he had presented himself well. He had provided all the right answers to the questions they asked, and he seemed quite technically capable. In fact, they were fairly confidant they would go ahead and hire him, but they decided to ask us to check his references—just to be sure.

During my conversation with the candidate's very first reference, I asked the question, "How would you characterize so-and-so's main strength on the job?" There was a long pause.

The reply was, "Well, actually his main strength was interviewing."

"Oh, really? Tell me what you mean."

The reference continued, "We went through all the standard steps with him, he presented himself well, provided all the right answers to the questions we asked, and seemed very knowledgeable about the technical aspects of the job. So we hired him. It took us about six months to discover he could only do about half the things he claimed he could."

At that point, I had to ask, "Did you talk to any previous employers about him before he was hired?"

The answer came, "No, but how I wish we *had*! The total price tag for that bad hiring decision was over $100,000!" (It should be noted, too, that the other references with whom we spoke similarly confirmed the comments cited.)

When we called our clients in Ohio (the prospective employers), you could almost hear their chins drop over the phone. They were prepared to pay this candidate over $85,000 in base salary, plus perks. If it had taken them six months to discover their error, it doesn't take a math whiz to figure out the potential cost to their company. Did careful reference checking help them avoid a very costly hiring mistake? Of course it did, and this real-life example clearly shows the *financial* value of careful reference checking. The potential damage to company or customer morale and the opportunity cost of passing over the *right* candidate is yet another matter and probably incalculable.

Following are some of the basic questions and issues this book addresses:

• The difference between a reference check and a
  background check

• Who should be checked

• Who should do the checking

♦ How to practically and lawfully check references

♦ How to lawfully respond to questions about former employees

♦ What questions should not be asked and, on the other side of the coin, what questions should not be answered

♦ What the most common misconceptions are

♦ What the legal issues (in everyday language) are

♦ How to assess the real value added when careful and consistent reference checking is brought to the hiring process

In addition, perhaps most convincingly, I'll relate some dandy horror stories about what can happen when references aren't checked. To any self-respecting manager, these should be stories even more frightening than a memo from the legal department advising all managers to, in effect, never risk getting out of bed!

In today's business climate, who can afford to stay in bed? When it comes to reference checking, this is a book on how to do it—practically, legally, and effectively.

# REFERENCE
# CHECKING
# FOR
# EVERYONE

# CHAPTER 1

# WHAT *IS* REFERENCE CHECKING?

## GETTING THE TERMS STRAIGHT

In the introduction to this book, I suggested that there isn't universal agreement among managers and human resouces (HR) people about the terminology used to describe the exercise of intelligently trying to ensure smart hiring decisions are being made. Frankly, I wish I had a dollar for every time I've talked to a prospective client, said that our business is reference checking, and heard the reply, "Oh, you mean doing background checks." Nope, that's *not* what I mean. A background check and a reference check are not the same thing—not by a long shot.

Other terms that muddy the waters of the preemployment process, just to mention a few, include *preemployment screening, candidate evaluation, employment verification*, and *credential screening*. Needless to say, there are all sorts of other combinations of terms that may or may not have anything to do with real reference checking. The point, of course, is that no single term is used by everyone consistently. This can be problematic.

Everybody knows what a plumber or electrician does; there is almost universal understanding of what those words mean and what services we can expect from those professionals. However, when we talk about reference checking, it's a bit like stirring up mud at the bottom of an otherwise tranquil pond. So, for purposes of this book, let's clearly define the terms we'll be using:

## Reference Check

A *reference check* is an objective evaluation of a candidate's past job performance, based on conversations with people who have actually worked with the candidate on a daily basis within the last five to seven years.

## Reference

A *reference* is a person with whom the candidate has actually worked. They may include current or former superiors, peers, and subordinates, depending on the situation. References can be either business or professional, depending on the occupation.

## Personal References

A *personal reference* is, by default, anybody else whom the candidate happens to know—a neighbor, a friend, or even a golfing buddy. Personal references, in other words, are people with whom the candidate has never worked.

Somehow, the concept of giving personal references has entered the lexicon of employment in a way that has long outlasted its practicality. In the days when hiring household servants was a common practice, for instance, it was good to have a reference who could vouch for a person's "character." The level of skill was not so much an issue as was the kind of individual you'd be bringing into the household. Today, good character (while still important) can be measured in many other ways than a list of personal friends or impressive-sounding clergy. Even for landlords, or people looking for a nanny for their children, the request for references should still be for *business* references. The landlord-tenant relationship is still a business relationship, as is the relationship between nannies and in-home health care workers and their employers. And that's how people evaluating prospective tenants, or nannies, or in-home health care workers should view it: as a business relationship. References, therefore, should still be people with whom the individual has actually worked—not people who would have no idea about the essential character of the individual in terms of things like honesty, punctuality, responsibility, or a dozen other qualities that only references who have had a *business* relationship with the candidate would know.

Unfortunately, "personal references" has become one of those overused catchphrases that disguises the *real* work of responsible, effective reference checking.

## Background Checks

The term *background check* is another catchall phrase that means checking the accuracy of basic information provided by a candidate for employment on a job application or résumé. Generally speaking, a background check, at least in my view, is a *threshold screening device*—primarily useful in making sure the candidate has not lied on his or her résumé or job application. A background check is an important step in the employee selection process, nevertheless, because it is a quick and relatively inexpensive way for the prospective employer to whittle down the pile of résumés or applications to only those candidates who are, at least, whom they claim to be. But remember, a background check is *not* an evaluation of past job performance. It is not a reference check. It is only a confirmation of information provided by the applicant on a résumé or job application.

Another thought on background checking versus reference checking: It would be unfair to leave the distinction between the two terms without some additional explanation. It is safe to say that background checks generally include verification of dates of employment, confirming both current and former job titles, verification of educational credentials, and verification of all professional licenses claimed.

Many employers also lump together doing a *credit check*, a *court check*, administering some sort of paper-and-pencil *aptitude* or *personality assessment test,* and sometimes *drug screening tests* under that heading of "background check." All of the terms noted previously are essentially some version of a background check, with very slight variations. For the purposes of this book, preemployment screening, candidate evaluation, employment verification, and candidate screening are all just additional ways of describing what I have chosen to call a background check.

While determining (via a background check) whether or not the candidate is, in fact, whom he or she claims to be is an important first step, that's all it really is—the first step. The second and far more important step is real reference checking. There is so much more to learn about a candidate for employment, or a prospective tenant, or even a nanny, before the decision can be made. And the only way to learn it is by talking to people who have worked with, rented to, or received service from the candidate or person in question.

## WHAT CAN BE LEARNED FROM CAREFUL REFERENCE CHECKS?

Careful reference checking could never be called an exact science; it is really more of an art. There are fundamental qualities that can be learned about a candidate for employment that really can be obtained in no other way.

Here's an example of how it works: A few years ago, I was asked to check the references of an individual who was being considered for a position as senior internal auditor for a major manufacturer.

All of his references were his friends, but they were also people with whom he had worked during the preceding few years at a major accounting firm in the Midwest. They reported that his overall performance had been outstanding and that he was a very responsible and capable individual who also had outstanding interpersonal skills. They expressed some concern, however, that he really wasn't quite ready for senior-level responsibility.

Their concern (which all three references expressed) was that if our client, the prospective employer, expected their friend and coworker to be able to perform the duties of a senior-level auditor from day one, he might indeed fail. First, this would throw the candidate seriously off his chosen career path, and second, the new employer's legitimate expectations would not be met. Now one might think such comments would have had a devastating effect on the candidate's chances with the new employer. But in fact the opposite turned out to be true. The prospective employer was sufficiently impressed with the overall performance of this guy, and they hired him anyway, but at a lower level. After about six months—after the man had time to get his feet on the ground and become familiar with the organization and the internal auditing function—he was promoted to the position for which he originally applied. It turned out to be a win-win situation for everybody. And that is exactly what reference checking is supposed to do: help ensure that the correct job match is made.

Here's another example that illustrates the point. We were asked to do a reference check on a candidate for a sound and vibration engineer's position. All three references described the candidate as extraordinarily skilled, very knowledgeable about his field of expertise, and able to work without much supervision or direction—once given a task to perform. But they intimated that his interpersonal skills were lacking, that he couldn't get along with anyone on the job, and that he had such an abrasive personality that other employees actually tried to avoid him. Again, one might assume that such an assessment would have killed this individual's chances of being hired. Not at all.

Armed with that knowledge beforehand, he was hired by the employer and, initially, assigned to an office where projects were essentially slid under the door for him to undertake. But the company also got him some interpersonal skill development training, and they reported back to us later that within about four months his ability to work effectively with others had enabled the company to promote him to a team leader position. By knowing in advance the areas of concern, the employer was able to address them and, in a very real way, increase this man's value to the company exponentially. Again, that's what real reference checking is all about.

I would even go so far as to suggest that there was no other way, in either example, for the prospective employers to have obtained this key information without carefully checking references beforehand. Just verifying that the candidate worked where he said he did or had the job title he claimed he had would not have provided this in-depth information. Even during the interviewing process, it is preposterous to assume these important concerns would have come up at all.

In the first instance, does anyone realistically believe the candidate for the senior internal auditor position would have said, "You know, I'm not sure I'm really ready to accept senior-level responsibility"? Or in the second example, how ridiculous is it to think the candidate for the sound and vibration engineer's position would have confessed, "Oh, by the way, I really annoy the people I work with because . . . well, I have a crummy personality"? Clearly, no other evaluative instrument would have produced the same result. A credit check certainly would not have revealed these issues, nor would a court check. The only way to obtain this *qualitative* information is through careful reference checking.

## The Importance of Multiple References

What can be learned through true reference checking is far more than most managers imagine. From the outset, it is important to keep in mind that the most reliable reference check involves not talking to a single reference, but ordinarily to *three*. Why? This is to enable the person reading the report to compare comments among references, to look for inconsistencies in responses to questions, and at the same time to validate various aspects of the candidate's performance over time and a variety of work-related situations. I have found, through the years, that often it is the *third* reference who solidifies and validates the overall reference report.

If there are disparities between the responses of two references, a tactful inquiry with a third reference often sheds exactly the right light needed to clear up the discrepancy. For instance, a comment about poor written communication skills from a reference who worked with the candidate five years ago compared with glowing remarks about the same thing from a current supervisor probably can be resolved by asking the third reference about the candidate's apparent improvement in this area.

I recall a case in point: The third reference simply explained the candidate's poor writing skills had been addressed in a performance review and the individual quickly signed up for a business communications course at a nearby community college. Not only did that explain the different responses, but it also suggested the candidate took to heart his need for improvement and did something about it.

Carefully checking references, therefore, will give the prospective employer a much clearer view of not only how well the candidate has performed in the past, but also how that performance relates to the job in question. It also has the potential to identify areas in which career development can take place. That's a triple benefit from carrying out one single task—reference checking.

It should be noted at this point that careful reference checking offers similar benefits in various other venues. Reference checking can be done by apartment managers on prospective tenants to ensure that they have a history of taking care of the property, paying rent on time—essentially whether or not they will be good renters. The same is true of any sort of service provider—a nanny for your children, a tutor, an in-home health care provider, or even a remodeling contractor. People who are seeking positions such as these should be happy to provide references—if they are all they claim to be. If they're not, keep looking. On the other side of the coin, failing to carefully check references in situations like these is far too great a risk to take with the safety of your children or loved ones who may need special help. Be sure to check references of *anyone* working in your home.

Here are a couple of other examples that illustrate the point. The wife of one of our best clients wanted to hire a nanny for her 9-year-old daughter. We were asked to check references on the leading candidate for the job, who, typically, had been recommended by a friend of a friend of a friend.

When we started contacting her references, it turned out that her closest experience to being a nanny was a one-month stint working in a day care center. Other references revealed that her longest tenure anywhere had been working in a florist shop for six months. The rest of her work history reflected very short periods of employment, termination from a variety of jobs, and no experience as a nanny.

In another instance, a client wanted to hire a chauffeur for his aged mother. The top candidate had been recommended by a friend. His references indicated that, at least, he had worked as a chauffeur and bodyguard before. His references also disclosed that he had an extensive military background and had been fired from more than one job for being too regimented in his ways. While working as a chauffeur and bodyguard, he had thrown the elderly man to the ground, breaking several ribs, because he thought he heard gunfire. It was a car backfiring! Perhaps he might have been an ideal candidate to protect a rock star but was hardly suitable as a chauffeur for a woman in her eighties.

## THE RISKS OF *NOT* DOING REFERENCE CHECKS: HORROR STORIES

Up to this point, I've offered some of the bright and sunny examples of what real reference checking is about and the real value it can add to the employee selection process. But I'm sure there are readers who are thinking, "Well, that's all very nice, but there are so many good candidates out there, and checking references sounds fairly labor-intensive (and even expensive). So why bother? Why not risk it?"

Well, let me share some of the horror stories that can happen when companies fail to check references. We'll talk about the legal implications of negligent hiring and negligent referral in later chapters, and when we do, it will be in plain straight-up English—no legalese. But for now, let's look at what can happen when employers just don't want "to bother."

Here's an example of what can happen when references *are* checked but the results ignored. A few years ago, we were asked to check references on a physician being considered for a staff position with an area hospital. At the outset, it should be noted that all the references with whom we spoke were actual colleagues of the candidate while he was in private practice. All three reported that the candidate had a drug problem, that he was undergoing weekly psychiatric care, and that they would not practice medicine with him again under any circumstances. At most, they said, he might be able to function as an ER physician, but only while being closely supervised. We submitted our report and, believe it or not, the hospital hired him anyway. Within six months, however, the state police arrested this physician and led him from the hospital in handcuffs for writing phony prescriptions for huge quantities of amphetamines and barbiturates. The out-of-pocket hospital cost for ignoring the information in the reference report: $100,000 plus.

Many may remember the case of Janet Cooke, who was hired by *The Washington Post* based solely on her impressive academic credentials. In other words, nothing in her professional background was checked. The newspaper only found out about her after she won a Pulitzer Prize for a story that was blatantly untrue. Not only was the story a fake, so was the writer.

Some time ago, a high-school dropout, who had been an Army medic, "borrowed" his cousin's academic credentials and successfully masqueraded as a doctor for three years before anyone bothered to check.

Another man was hired by a large company on the East Coast to handle their overseas operations. The employment decision was based solely on his interviewing skills and résumé. After a few months, his employers were wondering why he wasn't getting the job done. We were called in—after the fact—to check his references. As it turned out, the reason he wasn't getting the job done was because he had lied on his résumé not only about his accomplishments, but also about *ever* having done that type of work. The cost to the company for not checking: $150,000.

A few years ago, a woman was hired to be deputy budget director for the city of Aspen, Colorado. Nobody checked her references. Within a month she had diverted several thousand dollars to her personal checking account. Had references been checked, they would have revealed that she had been fired previously for doing exactly the same thing in New Mexico, and she had felony convictions for fraud and forgery.

Recently, at a major hospital in the Midwest, an anesthesiologist came into the surgical suite trying to eat a piece of pizza through his surgical mask. An after-the-fact reference check disclosed that the anesthesiologist had a substance abuse problem and had lost his license to practice medicine in three other states. The cost to the hospital for not checking: $125,000.

More recently was the high-profile case of George O'Leary, who was hired as head football coach at Notre Dame (for a day or so), until somebody discovered that he had falsified several of the accomplishments claimed on his résumé. A careful reference check could have easily avoided the embarrassing front-page headlines that resulted.

Not every horror story is without some small measure of humor. We were contacted several months ago by another large medical facility in Illinois. They were concerned that their new director of physical therapy wasn't living up to their expectations and they wanted us to verify, at least, his academic credentials. Eventually, we were supplied with an actual copy of his diploma from a college in Wales in Great Britain, which began in the usual way: "To all who shall see these presents, greetings: This is to certify that (so-and-so) has met all the requirements for (such-and-such) degree . . . ."

We sent the copy of the diploma to the registrar of the college and soon received a terse reply that began, "First of all, if this was a diploma from our college, it would have been written in *Latin*, not

11

English. We hope your client takes an equally dim view of this sort of prevarication." The cost of not checking: $75,000.

Finally, to illustrate that even hourly employees need to be checked, one of my account managers was doing a reference report on a candidate for a job as a construction worker. At the end of what seemed to be a fairly positive interview, the reference asked if we knew where the candidate might be found. Naturally, we didn't know, much to the disappointment of the reference, who added, "Gee, I was hoping you might know, 'cause he stole my truck when he left and the sheriff is still looking for him!"

## WHAT HAVE WE LEARNED?

To summarize, in this first chapter I've defined what reference checking is and made a clear distinction between real reference checking and doing a background check. I've identified other types of preemployment checks and noted how they are not the same, but are compliments to the reference-checking process. I've tried to demonstrate the breadth of information that can be obtained and graphically show the potential risks (and costs) of *not* checking. And finally, I've recounted some of the resulting horror stories, complete with a final touch of mirth.

# CHAPTER 2

# THE IMPORTANCE OF CAREFUL REFERENCE CHECKING

## DON'T LET FEAR OF A LAWSUIT STOP YOU FROM CHECKING REFERENCES

Here's an interesting experiment: Sneak up to the door of your human resources department (personnel, employment office, whatever it happens to be called where you are), shout out the word "LAWSUIT!" and then run away. The result will be something akin to setting a fox loose in the chicken coop. No other word seems to strike as much terror in the hearts of recruiters, human resource specialists, hiring managers, and others involved in the employee selection process as does the word *lawsuit*. Obviously, this silly example is nothing more than a demonstration of the sometimes irrational fears associated with our litigious society. But it illustrates an essential point about how far we've managed to drift from the fundamental common sense required in the hiring process.

Let's be really clear about this. Does it make any sense that a prospective employer shouldn't be free to talk openly with a job applicant's former employer about that candidate being considered for employment? It makes no sense at all. How else can the prospective employer *ever* objectively evaluate a candidate's past performance, experience, training, responsibilities, suitability for the job, and any number of other considerations? Is an employer stuck taking a candidate's word for everything? In a perfect world, a candidate for employment would always be totally forthcoming and honest about his or her skills and abilities—as well as his or her shortcomings. But unfortunately, the world isn't perfect—as some of the alarming examples in the previous chapter illustrate. Keep in mind, too, that people, even if they are being totally honest, seldom see themselves, in terms of their skills and abilities, as they are seen by others with whom they work.

Besides the possibility of not being honest about their skills, your potential employees could actually be hiding something. Yet people wonder whether an employer (or landlord) should be restricted to nothing more than verifying the information provided on a job application or supplied during an interview. Again, the reply must be, "Of course not." People who are afraid of delving into someone's background must remember that checking references and doing background checks has been, and continues to be, a *standard business practice.*

Can any responsible employer safely assume every word on a résumé or job application is true? And should any responsible employer base a hiring decision solely on the basis of the candidate's skill at interviewing? Another vote for "no."

Not only do reference checking and background checking make good business sense, the practice makes *common* sense, regardless of whether you're hiring a senior vice president, a restaurant food server, a home contractor, or a new family physician. Let's decide to get past the fear that somehow verifying the people we'd like to hire—regardless of the task or service to be performed—is somehow rude, a bad thing, or worse yet, illegal. It isn't, it never has been, and it never will be.

# WHAT ARE THE REAL RISKS?

Now that we're free of unnecessary guilt, I do want to mention that there are both real and imaginary risks associated with the whole reference-checking process. But don't panic. Let's take a common-sense look at these risks and balance them against the risks of not checking at all. (For those who need some official-sounding term to go with this, think of it as human resource risk management—very official sounding, don't you think?).

## *Should You Worry about Privacy Issues?*

It should go without saying that people seeking employment and housing have basic rights, just like everyone else. These rights aren't particularly associated with the hiring process, but are fundamental rights guaranteed by the Constitution of the United States. The particular right with which we're concerned at the moment is Amendment IV from the original Bill of Rights, which has to do with Protection from Unreasonable Search and Seizure. Since 1791, the Supreme Court has been defining and redefining what Amendment IV actually means. The process by which all that has taken place over the past 200-plus years is pretty dull stuff for the average reader. But it all boils down to the right to be free from unreasonable search and seizure. This has evolved into a fundamental right to privacy, and that's all we really need to know about its origin.

We all have a right to our privacy, and it is that right to privacy that really goes to the heart of any legal risks associated with reference checking. At this level of analysis (we'll get to related issues later), there are almost no risks associated with checking references and virtually no risks at all associated with checking public records.

But before going further, let's address the commonsense approach to public verses private as it relates to what we can find out about each other in the workplace. The most fundamental illustration might be the information (available and published) on our elected representatives in the political sphere. The courts have defined some information as "public" and other information as "private."

The difference has to do with court proceedings. Amendment VI in the Bill of Rights guarantees all of us, as we would want it to, the right to a "speedy and public trial." In other words, all trials in this country are public. Therefore, the records of all court proceedings are public. So, if the aforementioned politician had ever been arrested and convicted of anything, by definition, it is a public proceeding and anybody, and I mean *anybody*, is allowed to walk into the county courthouse, or wherever the proceedings took place, and check it out. There is nothing you or anybody else can do to prevent that from happening, because it is a *public record*.

On the other hand, our politician's medical records are private and *nobody* can gain access to those records.

"Ah-ha," you say. "I just applied for life insurance, and they wanted to know my medical history. How private is that?" Well, the simple answer is that if you don't want the insurance company to have access to your medical records, you can always say no. But if you do that, don't expect that insurance company to insure you, either. Nobody is going to take it on faith alone that you're in good health. That's why life insurance companies insist on being given *permission* to check your medical records.

Now we're down to the key distinction between public records and private records. No record is really private, no matter what the law may say, if you give someone else *permission* to access that otherwise private record. When we apply for life insurance, if we want it, we ordinarily give the prospective underwriter permission to check our medical records. That's our choice. We could always say no. But how much sense does that really make?

The same is true for reference checking. Ordinarily, talking to previous employers about a former employee's job performance, in the strictest sense, could be an invasion of privacy. But if we want to continue to be considered for employment, most of us will give the prospective employer permission to talk to the people for whom we've worked. And why wouldn't we? If we've performed well, gotten favorable performance reviews, and worked well with others on the job, why wouldn't we want a prospective employer to know that?

The bottom line is this: Most of us are willing to give up some of our privacy rights in exchange for things we want, like getting life insurance or, more to our point, getting a job or a place to live. So from the prospective employer's standpoint, what are the risks of checking references? None, if the employer simply *asks* the candidate for permission to do so.

## The Potential Risks Vary Greatly

Now, what are the legal risks associated with *not* checking references? In the last chapter, I offered some real-life examples of what can happen as the result of not checking references. Yet, other than the occasional horror story, what are the more fundamental risks of not checking? The most basic risk, of course, is making a poor hiring decision—failing to hire the right person for the job to be done. For the landlord, it means getting a tenant who isn't responsible. Proving that a candidate is all he or she claims to be, while being useful and seemingly fundamental information, merely tells the prospective employer that the candidate hasn't lied on his or her résumé or job application. It says *nothing* about the candidate's ability to do the job. Clearly, there is no other way to determine if the candidate is right for the job *without* checking references.

Some HR people will argue that their skill and experience at interviewing is sufficient to make a determination of suitability for the job, but even the most skilled interviewer cannot avoid allowing subconscious impressions to color his or her view of a candidate. Some people just naturally hit it off; others don't. That brief symbiotic relationship, or the lack of it, doesn't say anything about the candidate's ability to do the job either. And, we all know some people's primary talent seems to be their ability to sell themselves.

The other risks associated with not checking references include the following:

- Hiring people who really aren't who or what they claim to be
- Damaging the company's ability to function normally
- Inflicting potential damage to the company's reputation
- Suffering loss of valued customers—past and future
- Possibly contributing to the development or delivery of a defective—even dangerous—product

I recall one particularly egregious example a few years ago when we were asked to simply verify the academic credentials of an individual being considered for a research chemist's position with our client, a manufacturer of medical testing equipment. The individual claimed to have earned a degree in chemistry from a major Midwestern university. A quick call to the registrar's office disclosed that the individual not only had failed to complete the work for the degree, but he'd also been dismissed early for poor academic performance. This person's prior employment had been with a major pharmaceutical firm. One can only imagine the potential harm that could have been done if that person had been involved with the development of a new medication that caused medical injury or even loss of life!

Would the legal settlement have been in the millions of dollars? Probably. The point is, nobody bothered to check and see whether or not the degree claimed had been earned.

On balance, then, which set of risks is greater? Being accused of invasion of privacy (which can easily be avoided by getting written permission to contact references and conduct a background check)? Or is there a bigger risk involved with hiring someone who, at the very least, is unqualified for the job and, at the worst, is an outright fraud? The answer should be obvious.

## MAKING SURE YOU HIRE THE RIGHT PERSON FOR THE JOB—THE FIRST TIME

It probably isn't possible to guarantee you will never make a hiring mistake. But developing and implementing a preemployment screening process that is consistently followed will significantly reduce your risk.

There are essentially two ways to look at adopting a candidate screening process:

♦ It can be viewed as a critical investment in the long-term success of your company. Remember, the company is really no better than the people who are employed by it.

♦ You can think of it as nothing more than a perfunctory way for your company to protect itself. By being able to prove "something" was done prior to making a job offer, you can avoid the possibility of being sued for negligent hiring (which we'll discuss in detail later).

Obviously, the first option is the most practical way to view candidate screening. But many companies still take the second view,

19

and many more companies ignore the process altogether. What so many companies fail to realize is that by taking the first view, they are, by default, also taking care of the second. In other words, a good background and reference-checking system will reduce the likelihood of costly hiring mistakes, on the one hand, and clearly demonstrate, to anyone who cares to look, that reasonable care was exercised in the hiring process. Simultaneously, you've effectively eliminated the specter of negligent hiring litigation.

Meanwhile, the woods are full of all kinds of tools that are supposed to help employers make good hiring decisions. The most obvious is the structured job interview, which is indeed the key way to pick your top choices. Others include a wide variety of paper-and-pencil aptitude and personality tests that measure just about any human quality or characteristic you'd care to name. We've already talked about background checks, and we'll come back to those later. A variety of drug screening tests is also available. Outside search firms supposedly provide insight into the skills and potential of the job candidates they recommend. And then there's reference checking. Among all the previously mentioned options, I firmly believe that carefully evaluating *past* job performance is the best way to measure *future* job performance— that's all there is to it.

Careful reference checking carries with it four distinct benefits:

♦ It provides an in-depth look at past job performance.

♦ It allows the prospective employer to evaluate how the candidate's skills, experience, training, education, and overall performance fit the requirements of the job to be filled.

♦ If done properly, it highlights areas in which the candidate can improve or gain additional experience to increase his or her value to the employer over time.

 * It clearly demonstrates that care was consistently and fairly used in the employee selection process.

## The Potential Costs of Hiring the Wrong Person

I had a very unusual conversation with an HR manager just a few months ago. We were talking about the value of careful reference and background checking, and I was asked what it would cost to do a thorough reference check. I replied that, depending on the position, it could range anywhere from under $100 to as much as $500.

The response was, "Oh, we'd never spend that much just to check references. As a matter of fact, we're very proud that our average total cost-per-hire is less than $300." Clearly, this HR manager missed the point of the basic "risk test" we described earlier.

Later, that same hiring manager asked if we could do exit interviews. I said we could, and I asked him what their annual turnover might be.

"Oh, nearly 40 percent," was the answer. I didn't bother to reply; he wasn't listening anyway. But I was thinking, "Look, have you stopped to think what it's costing your company to replace 4 out of 10 workers every 12 months? You're spending more to replace—not to mention train—those people than you would *ever* spend if you were more careful about who you hired in the first place!" Talk about being penny-wise and pound-foolish!

Having done an extensive survey of our own existing clients, we have learned that the actual out-of-pocket cost of hiring the wrong person for the job, regardless of the reason, is *three times the annual salary for that position!* In other words, if the job pays $50,000 per year, the total cost associated with hiring the wrong person (including all the costs associated with replacing that person) will be approximately $150,000! This amount is calculated by adding up the preemployment costs, such as running ads and bring-ing in candidates for interviews, along with the costs of preemploy-ment screening, the amount of salary and benefits already paid out, plus the costs of duplicating that entire exercise again to find a replacement. And that figure does not include the less obvious costs that can accrue from loss of business, damage to your company's reputation, and the potential harm to morale of the people within your organization. All of those costs added together could make the results of our survey actually turn out to be *low*!

The point, simply restated, is that it's far less expensive to ensure you're hiring the best person possible the first time around. The smart strategy, therefore, is to do everything possible to make the most informed hiring decision possible, rather than run the risk of a seat-of-the pants hire that could backfire and cost big bucks.

## NEGLIGENT HIRING—CAUGHT BETWEEN A ROCK AND A HARD PLACE

What is negligent hiring? Simply put, *negligent hiring* is the failure on the part of an employer to use *reasonable care* in the selection of employees that results in harm to an innocent third party. OK, what does the term *reasonable care* mean within the context of the employment process? One classic definition would be that degree of care is what an ordinarily reasonable and prudent person would exercise under the same circumstances to avoid putting innocent third parties at risk of harm. Now, what do we mean by *harm*? Is it just physical harm, such as violence in the workplace? No. Harm, within this context, can mean financial harm, harming a customer by producing a defective product, or even harming another's repu-tation and good name in the marketplace.

Will the standard of care the employer needs to exercise be the same for every position? No. Why? Because the risk of harm will vary according to the type of position at issue. Obviously, a higher standard of care is required if you're hiring an airline pilot than if you're hiring a fry cook.

But before we go into that, here's a real-life example of what can happen when reasonable care *isn't* used. A high school in the Midwest was sued for negligent hiring, among other things, by the parents of a child who was molested by a teacher. There was no question about the facts; the teacher was caught in the act by an administrator. Even though the  teacher was fired, the parents sued, claiming the school had failed to use reasonable care in the hiring process. This negligence was based on the fact that the teacher had, as it turned out, a history of child molestation. And the parents claimed this could easily have been discovered if the school had done a reference check and a court check. Sadly, the claim proved true. The teacher had a prior conviction of child molestation in another state where he had worked before. The school hadn't checked anything! The teacher involved simply submitted his résumé, the building principal and the assistant superintendent conducted two interviews, and a job offer was made.

The parents proved the school had been negligent because a "reasonable employer" would have—at the very least—done a court check to make sure the candidate (who would have supervisory responsibility over students) had no history of errant behavior. The trial court awarded the parents over a million dollars in damages as a result of the school's failure to use reasonable care. They were guilty, in other words, of negligent hiring. The school's negligence is obvious.

So, let's recap. Are you doomed if you do a background and reference check on the people you hire? Nope. Can you hurt yourself or your business if you don't check? Maybe. So why take any chance in the first place? The logical thing to do is require candidates for employment to submit a complete work history, provide appropriate references, and sign a comprehensive waiver granting the prospective employer specific permission to not only verify the information on the résumé, but also to contact references. Carrying out those three simple steps accomplishes two important objectives:

- It ensures that people are who they claim to be—and that they can do what they claim they can do.
- It proves the employer did, in fact, use reasonable care in the employee selection process.

The net effect is to improve hiring practices and avoid any possible accusation of negligent hiring.

## Negligent Rental Tenants—Who Is Responsible for Damages?

In rental situations, risk management can easily become a nest of snakes. It's all in the wording. Generally speaking, the party responsible is (or should be) clearly defined in the contract or lease agreement signed by the landlord and the tenant. The very least a landlord can expect, however, is that the dwelling will be left in no worse condition than it was in when the tenant moved in—with the exception of ordinary wear and tear. What will constitute "ordinary wear and tear" is, more than anything else, a matter of common sense and how clearly those terms are defined in the lease agreement. Most standard leases specify that the tenant is expected to maintain the property in good repair. But a fair lease is not all one-sided. Some leases require the landlord to make routine repairs; others place that burden on the tenant.

Some leases allow the tenant to put up new wallpaper, paint, or install carpet. Others forbid that sort of thing, which means that the landlord may be obliged to do all or some of those things—not at the tenant's whim—but under very specific circumstances as defined in the lease.

Negligence, in terms of rental agreements, can move in both directions. It all depends on the terms of the lease. Damage caused by the tenant, beyond anything contained in the lease, clearly will be the responsibility of the tenant to repair. The same is true, on the other hand, for the landlord. If he or she has agreed to be responsible for providing heat and fails to keep the furnace in good working order, for instance, and the tenant's property is harmed in some way as a result, the landlord is liable. But these issues aren't so much a matter of "negligence" as they are a matter of violating terms and conditions in the lease.

Negligence, as far as damage to leased property goes, will always fall on the party whose failure to act caused the damage—and that isn't always the tenant. For instance, if the tenant negligently fails to lock the door and the premise is vandalized, the tenant would be held responsible. On the other hand, if the landlord has failed to fix the lock, the burden for paying for the repairs would probably fall on the landlord.

The key, however, to avoiding many of these problems (if you're the landlord) is to clarify the wording in your lease agreement. You may want to pass the document by your attorney for review. Another option is to insist that prospective tenants provide a list of previous landlords from whom I've leased or rented property and obtain express permission from the prospective tenant to contact them. We'll talk about how best to do that in subsequent chapters.

In this chapter we talked about the plain old common sense that justifies the reference-checking exercise. We compared the risks of checking references with the significantly greater risks associated

with *not* checking. We reviewed the costs of making bad hiring decisions. We looked at the ways to increase the likelihood of hiring the
right person—the *first* time. Then we took a practical look at the
concept of negligent hiring, and we explored some of the fundamental aspects of the landlord-tenant relationship.

In the next chapter, we'll look at one of the most critical questions
associated with the whole employee selection process: Who should
be checked and why?

# CHAPTER 3

# WHO SHOULD BE CHECKED—AND WHY

## EVERYBODY SHOULD BE CHECKED!

The honest answer to the question of who should be reference checked is simple: Everybody. And while that may seem like a flippant answer, it is offered as a sound, sensible, and fundamental truth. Even in informal, everyday life situations, we do a fair amount of checking—and don't even realize we're doing it. If you need any sort of household repairs done, my guess would be that many of you ask friends or relatives or neighbors: "Who do you use?" "What do you think about so-and-so?" Or "What has your experience been using this person or that?" How many of you have asked others for their opinion when looking for a new hairstylist or barber: "Who does a good job?" "What do they charge?" Or just generally, "Do you like them?"

When you stop to think about it, we do the same sort of thing for nearly every type of human interaction we encounter, from our dealings with the neighborhood auto mechanic to booking a concert zitherist to even a blind date. We "ask around." All that asking around is really a form of reference checking.

Obviously, seeking a simple consensus of approval is not as formalized as the type of reference checking we've been talking about up to now, but the point should be clear that we do a lot more reference checking than we may think we do. All of us talk to friends, coworkers, relatives, neighbors, and others about nearly every conceivable type of provider of goods or services accessible in the marketplace. "Who has the best prices on stereos?" "Is your dentist taking new patients these days?" "Which car dealer do you like?" We're checking references, albeit informally, all the time.

Therefore, isn't it amazing that we fret and fume about the propriety of checking references on the people we're planning to hire? Regardless of whether it's a new six-figure CEO or a part-time security guard, employers seem perplexed about not only whether references should be checked, but also about how to go about it. And yet, those same employers will make several thorough inquiries before settling on a new pediatrician for their children.

To further illustrate the point, I recall a couple of instances where carefully checking references on just these sorts of people helped avoid serious hiring mistakes. We did a reference and background check on a candidate for a security guard's position, and the court check revealed the individual had numerous convictions for the illegal possession of automatic weapons and explosives!

Another example involved a candidate for a high-salaried CEO's position. A major client on the East Coast was very seriously considering this man for its top position because he had impressed the hiring committee as being a strong, energetic leader who could take them to the next level of corporate success. We were asked to prepare a reference report. Although the individual had a long and distinguished career as a very accomplished corporate executive, all three of his references essentially said that for about the last five years, the man had been coasting, living on his past laurels. They even intimated that he had been circulating his résumé in hopes of hitting one more big lick, in terms of compensation and benefits, before comfortably sliding into retirement. This was hardly the profile of a man still energized and prepared to take the prospective employer where they hoped to go.

As a final illustration, we were asked to check the references for a family practice physician for a small-town hospital that was desperate to bring a new doctor to town. The reference report revealed that the physician being wined and dined by the local hospital board was, in fact, the defendant in multiple malpractice lawsuits! The interesting twist to the story is that the physician had already moved to town and was in the process of opening his downtown office. My senior vice president, who had personally done the reference report, said she would bet it wouldn't be long before he left town. And within less than a month, he was gone. He had departed in the middle of the night, and the only tangible evidence that he had ever been in town was his new sign lying on the sidewalk outside his former office.

## *Three Occupations Where Reference Checking Should Be a High Priority*

This last example brings me to one of my major concerns surrounding the whole question of who should be checked. Over the past two decades, my office staff has noticed there are three specific occupational groups that do the least amount of careful background and job performance-based reference checking. And if you work in these professions, pay careful attention to this discussion. They are health care, banking, and public education. Surprised? Even shocked? If you're not, perhaps you should be. What, after all, is more important to each of us than our health, our financial security, and the safety of our children? Put another way, what three key occupations require more trust from us? Is it important to know more about the people employed in our health care, banking, and public education, or is it okay to know less? Point made.

Previously, I've given you several examples of health-care-related horror stories involving malpractice, substance abuse, and falsifying medical credentials. They represent only a tip of the lurking iceberg that is our current health care crisis. Part of the problem, clearly, is the critical shortage of all sorts of health care providers in nearly every field, due, in part, to the aging of the vast baby boom generation.

It seems that every day there is some new revelation about nursing home employees abusing the elderly. Is there any legal obligation on behalf of nursing homes to do any sort of reference checking on the people responsible for providing essential care for one or both of your parents and, maybe someday, you? You may be surprised to learn the current answer is "nope."

Must public schools do any sort of mandated performance-based reference check on teachers, administrators, and other school personnel? These, by the way, are people who are responsible for the education—and safety—of your children. The answer is still "nope." Why not? you ask. It is because in education, like in health care, the demand for personnel (in this case, teachers and administrators) far exceeds the present supply. There are simply too few licensed administrators to go around. Also, salaries for beginning teachers are notoriously low. Nonteaching jobs, assuming they aren't volunteer positions, typically pay lower still. Schools, in many instances, have had to turn to volunteer coaches and assistant coaches in order to field teams. Are any of these people checked in any meaningful way that will provide some measure of protection for our children? The answer once again is "more than likely not."

Most school administrators will counter that they have no budgets for thorough checking, or they'll say it's too time-consuming or they lack the resources to do the work. And besides, they add, "We're so desperate to fill these vacancies, we feel we're lucky to find anybody willing to do the job at all." One must ask, at what price, in terms of the safety of our children?

Not long ago I was talking with a vice president of human resources of a major multistate financial institution. I asked if his company did any sort of reference checking on their tellers. "Are you kidding?" was his reply. "How could we justify checking references on our tellers when we don't pay them that much and we have significant turnover among tellers anyway." Talk about short-sighted! Who represents the bank to the majority of its customers? Is it the senior loan officer in the carpeted office upstairs? She may account for higher numbers of the bank's total assets, but it's the teller who personifies the bank to the most customers. Wouldn't you think it might be worthwhile to spend a few bucks to find out if a teller candidate is honest and to learn whether or not that person gets along well with others and can remain calm and polite in frequently stressful situations? As I listened to that VP rationalize not checking the references of teller candidates, I couldn't help wondering how many customers he has already lost because of a teller's unpleasant personality. How many former customers might have been kept, how many new loans and mortgages would have come their way if only a little time had been invested in the selection of honest and personable first-line employees?

Hiring mistakes within financial institutions can also take place in the rarified atmosphere of the boardroom. A couple of years ago, a member of the board of directors of a multistate bank hired a senior vice president without telling anybody or checking anything. The new hire was an old college buddy of the director's, and it wasn't questioned by the bank's HR people for fear of insulting the director. (Rank has its privileges.) Within six months the new VP had secretly transferred something like a quarter of a million dollars to his own private offshore account. Was there serious fallout from this hiring disaster? You bet! The director was forced to resign, the top people in HR were fired, and the bank lost millions in deposits from customers whose confidence in the institution had been totally shattered.

Health care, banking, and public education. Your health, your money, and the safety of your children . . . Too much time? Too much trouble? Too expensive? *Now* is the time for the answer to be a resounding "nope!" If you've been tempted to do a light reference check, or even pass on the reference check altogether, hopefully these stories have convinced you of the crucial need for reference checking.

## PROBLEMS CAUSED BY LACK OF PROSECUTION

A problem you may encounter during the reference-checking process is the unfortunate fact that people are rarely prosecuted for crimes they commit on the job. Having served two terms on a board of education, I have seen first-hand what can happen when teachers, coaches, or other school employees become inappropriately involved with students. They are given two choices: resign or be fired. Which alternative do you think they pick? They resign, of course. But does the problem then really go away? When resignation is allowed to be the only community response, seldom is any legal prosecution done, and therefore no court record is created of the event. Then, later on down the time line, some other school system and, even more importantly, some other child pays a terrible price. So, even if the new school corporation does a court check on its candidates for employment, what do you think they'll find? Nothing. Because no one was ever prosecuted, no court record will be found. So, the former employee in question goes right back into the classroom, or to the playing field, or the custodial position with the next school corporation with a "clean" record.

Even if the next school corporation does a cursory confirmation of previous jobs held and, by chance, should ask why the candidate left, the only response will be "resignation." What is seldom, if ever, asked is, "Could this person have stayed?" or "Would you hire this person again?"

Within public education there is another facet to this problem that needs to be discussed: How do schools get rid of an incompetent teacher who for whatever reason isn't performing well? What if this individual hasn't actually reached the legal definition of "incompetent, immoral, or insubordinate," which, by the way, are the only legal conditions under which a tenured teacher can be fired. Again, as a former school board member, I can attest to the belief among school administrators that the best way to get rid of a poor teacher is to sing his or her praises and hope he or she moves on to another school. In other words, schools feel their only option is to give a poor performer a glowing reference in order to get rid of that problem. But once again, careful reference checking, initiated by the school doing the hiring, would probably produce significant red flags that would keep the poor performer from being foisted off on another school corporation. Later in this book, we'll look at what you can do to detect red flags and how to follow through on any potential problem of which you become aware.

## Is Legislation the Answer?

Is public pressure being exerted on banks or schools or hospitals— or any business in general—to more carefully check the people they hire? Sometimes there is—when a fresh horror story hits the news. But the pressure soon fades when public attention is distracted by some new story, and the inertia dissipates until the next crisis occurs.

The main problem stems from the following factors:

- A lack of understanding about how to do thorough reference checking
- A general unwillingness to take the time or invest the resources in developing a consistent preemployment process
- A preconceived belief that checking might be too costly

What is so sad about this situation is that if more employers made careful reference checking an integral part of their hiring practices, many of these undesirables would be discouraged from applying for employment in the first place—knowing their previous misdeeds probably would be revealed.

## CHECK BOTH ENDS OF THE SPECTRUM— AND EVERYONE IN BETWEEN

Over the last two decades, during which I've been in the reference-checking business, my staff and I have witnessed a very interesting phenomenon. Simply stated, it's the tendency of some companies to assiduously check the most senior hires within the organization and ignore the hourly workforce. We've seen companies spend thousands of dollars to prepare a dossier on their top-level candidates on one hand, then do nothing more than interview their hourly candidates. Afterward, they wonder why annual turnover within the hourly ranks exceeds 30 percent.

At the other extreme are companies who carefully scrutinize the lowest-paid people with every sort of background check imaginable and, at the high end, take every word on the résumé of a candidate for the CEO's position as gospel. It almost seems as if there exists something of an elite class of job seeker whose credentials appear to be so impeccable that to check them would be perceived an insult to the candidate. Doctors tend to fall within this elite class, but the handful of horror stories I've already provided should prove that not every physician is a saint.

The point, of course, is that job applicants at both ends of the spectrum, not to mention the middle, should have their references checked. I recall another recent illustration that supports the point very well. The chief executive with the Indiana Public Employee's Retirement Fund hired an individual for one of the top jobs within his agency, a position that gave the candidate access to the personal financial records of thousands of current and former state employees, as well as their social security numbers. The only preemployment check that was conducted was a once-over-lightly court check. Basically, as far as anyone can tell, the executive doing the hiring simply liked the guy and wanted to hire him for the job. (That sort of thing happens in and around the corporate boardroom more times than most people would imagine). *The Indianapolis Star*, a major metropolitan newspaper acting on an anonymous tip, discovered that this individual had worked for a similar public employee retirement fund in an adjoining state and had a felony conviction on his record for identity theft! Not only that—this person had actually spent time in jail and had lost his license to practice law! To make a long story short, the individual was arrested again for identity theft, and two of the top three executives with the fund were fired. We were asked by the local media if we could have discovered that the candidate was not all he claimed to be. And my response was, "Sadly, yes. This tragedy was completely preventable. The first thing we would have done was confirm that the man was licensed to practice law in this state." He claimed he had his license to practice law in Indiana. "That would have been our first red flag that something was wrong. One felony conviction would have precluded him from obtaining a license to practice law," I told the reporter.

(There would have been other red flags, too, if anybody had bothered to check his references).

More recently, a temp employee had somehow gained access to the personal information of current and retired state employees within the same agency. He was arrested for—guess what?—identity theft.

The point is this: Everyone within an organization should have his or her references checked. This includes not just the top people, but also everyone else down the line, including the temps.

As a general rule, the more shallow the pool of available talent, at every level, the greater the tendency for employers to neglect checking references because they're so desperate to fill vacancies with a warm body and get on with the work. The irony is that the more shallow the candidate pool, the greater the need to carefully check references. Why? Well, it might be telling to investigate why the talent pool is shallow in the first place. A pessimistic (but not unreasonable) explanation might be that the talent pool is shallow because only a few persons in this line of work have avoided a criminal record to date. For some job descriptions, this is not unrealistic. How many employers want to be the first to have a convicted felon on the payroll? This is also why performance-based reference checking is so important during periods approaching full employment, or when the candidate pool within a specific occupational group is unusually shallow.

But then, during periods of *high unemployment*, the necessity for careful reference checking is equally great. The more people who are out there looking for work, the more likely they are to feel they need a competitive edge to land a scarce job. Therefore, fudging on academic credentials or exaggerating former responsibilities and achievements is an extreme temptation.

So, does my initial response to the question at the start of this chapter—who should be checked?—really merit a response of "everybody"? Clearly, yes. And as for the second question—why?— I have this advice: To those responsible for hiring people—regardless of your occupational field, regardless of your skills and past experience—the job you save could be your own.

# CHAPTER 4

# HOW TO CHECK REFERENCES

## CHOOSING REFERENCES AND GETTING PERMISSION

### *The Candidate's Responsibility to Provide a Range of References*

One of the most common errors people make when checking references is underestimating the role of the candidate in the employee selection process. There is a presumption that once the candidate has submitted a résumé or filled out a job application, his or her job is done.

For those employers who also ask the candidate to provide references, there is also another presumption that they're stuck with the names the candidate provides. That second presumption, by the way, goes right to the core belief held by many employers that checking the references provided by the candidate is a waste of time. "Why would a candidate ever supply the names of references who would ever say anything bad about him?" we often hear. "So what good are they?" In other words, many hiring managers believe candidate-provided references aren't going to help the prospective employer evaluate the candidate because they'll always say good things. (Knowing what to ask and how to ask it, however, will make these references more valuable, but more on that later.)

If people making hiring decisions see themselves, figuratively speaking, as being held hostage by the candidate's choice of references, then calling them probably *is* a waste of time. But there is a simple solution to this problem that will not only increase the prospects of references offering useful job performance information but also cause candidates, who may not be all they claim, to withdraw from further consideration.

Put the responsibility on the *candidate* to come up with the type of references *you* want. The easiest way to accomplish this is to establish a policy mandating that before any job offer can be made, references must be checked. More importantly, tell prospective employees that it is company policy to check references and you would like references who fit the following description:

+ At least three people with whom the candidate has actually worked, on a daily basis, within the last five to seven years— for a period not less than six months.

+ At least one former superior, one coworker, and if possible, one subordinate. (Clearly, not every candidate can come up with that exact mix of references, but most candidates should be able to come up with coworkers and a boss or two.)

+ It also should be made clear to the candidate that references will be called. Make sure the candidate understands that not only should the references be expecting a call, but they should also be willing to answer the questions asked.

In short, require the candidate to come up with his or her own references, and clearly define the types of references you want. Do not automatically accept any reference the candidate wants to give you.

Taking this approach solves other problems. First, it practically guarantees candidates will, if they haven't already done so, ask the appropriate people to serve as references. In other words, they will have gotten permission to list these people as references. Furthermore, the mere act of asking dramatically increases the likelihood that references will talk about the candidate to a prospective employer—because, more than likely, they will be expecting the call.

By the same token, if they're not willing to answer questions about the candidate, why would they agree to be a reference in the first place? More importantly, if they decline to discuss the candidate for whom they've agreed to serve as a reference, a major red flag should immediately go up in the mind of the prospective employer. Taken from another perspective (that of the job seeker), why would you ever list someone as a reference without asking the person first or without finding out up front if he or she will talk to a prospective employer?

## A Common Problem: The Employee Has Had the Same Manager for Several Years

Occasionally, job seekers will say that they've only worked for one employer for the last decade and they don't want that employer to know they're looking for other employment. This has to be respected. One of the unwritten codes in the reference-checking business is to never jeopardize anyone's current job. By the same token, for individuals who have a lengthy history with one employer, it defies imagination that during all that time, they haven't made friends with at least three people with whom they've also worked who wouldn't be willing to confidentially serve as references—company policy notwithstanding. From the job seeker's standpoint, long-tenured employees also need to remember that excellent references do things like retire, take other jobs, move to other functional areas within the same organization, or relocate to another physical plant owned by the company. In other words, a serious candidate can come up with appropriate references 99.9 percent of the time. On those occasions where a candidate says he or she simply cannot provide references to a prospective employer, my advice would be to look for someone else to fill the job.

Know the "statute of limitations." This isn't intended as a legalism, but rather as confirmation of the notion that all references should be people with whom the candidate has worked within the last five to seven years. Why? Talking to a reference from 10 years ago is really testing that person's memory. Also, people change over time; they gain experience, learn new things, become more professional, and so on. I would hate to think that my employability today hinged on what somebody with whom I worked a decade ago happened to remember about me!

## Waivers and Permission, Express and Implied

In Chapter 3, we talked about having all candidates sign a comprehensive waiver granting permission to prospective employers to contact their references. To bring the importance of that exercise into sharper focus, let's talk about what express and implied waivers are.

A *waiver* and a *release* mean essentially the same thing and are normally signed statements whereby the person seeking employment gives away his or her right to privacy in exchange for the opportunity to gain employment. By signing a waiver/release, the job seeker is essentially saying, "I understand that I am giving up my right to privacy in exchange for the chance to get a job." That does not mean, however, that the prospective employer has the right to probe into every aspect of a job seeker's life. Normally, what the employer may do is clearly defined by the language contained in the waiver and nothing more. Here's an example of a waiver:

## NOTICE, AUTHORIZATION, AND RELEASE
## REGARDING CONSUMER REPORT
## AND INVESTIGATIVE CONSUMER REPORT

**Notice to Applicant/Employee:** As part of the Company's pre-employment screening process, the Company may obtain a consumer report *or investigative consumer report* with respect to an applicant for employment or current employee. The consumer report will not be used for any other purpose. *If an investigative consumer report, as defined by the Fair Credit Reporting Act (FCRA), is prepared, the applicant may request a copy of this report and a written summary of rights under the FCRA.*

**Scope of Report:** The undersigned understands that the investigation may inquire into records that include, but are not limited to, consumer credit history, criminal records, driving records, education records, employment records such as performance evaluations and attendance reports, general public records, and other related records. These records may include information as to the undersigned's character, work habits, performance, and experience, along with reasons for termination of past employment. The undersigned understands that this report may also include information obtained from various government agencies that maintain records relating to driving, credit history, criminal activity, civil issues, administrative issues, and other matters, as well as claims involving the undersigned in the files of insurance companies. The undersigned also understands that this report may also include information obtained directly from individuals or past employers that may be helpful in making an employment decision.

**Applicant/Employee's Authorization and Release:** The undersigned has read and understands the above. The undersigned hereby authorizes, without reservation, the Company or any party or agency contracted by the Company to obtain a consumer report regarding him/her. The undersigned hereby releases the Company, its agents, and employees from any liability in connection with their use of the report or their reliance thereon in connection with any decision made by them. The undersigned also releases any person or employer from any liability that may arise as a result of furnishing any requested information pursuant to this form.

This form, in original or copy, shall be valid for this and any future reports or updates that may be requested.

Signature of Applicant or Employee _____

Date_____ Print Full Name _____

Obviously, the preceding waiver does not give the prospective employer permission to peek in the job seeker's window or ask the neighbors about his or her lifestyle on weekends. It is a precise statement of exactly what the prospective employer needs to know to make a more informed employment decision—that is, the candidate's ability to do the job, and nothing more.

Now let's talk about the difference between an *implied* waiver and an *express* waiver.

* **Implied waiver**. It is a well-established principle that the mere act of applying for a job, of submitting a job application or a résumé that includes a list of references, is an implied waiver of the right to privacy regarding employment history and job performance. Courts have held that there is a presumption that the information voluntarily provided by a job seeker may be checked by the prospective employer, because it is a long-standing and standard business practice.

- **Express waiver.** The express waiver is a signed release by the candidate. The only difference between an implied waiver and an express waiver is that the express waiver is a written statement that the job seeker actually signs.

Technically, there is a third type of waiver—a verbal one.

- **Verbal waiver.** If the prospective employer does nothing more than ask the permission of the candidate to check the information provided on the job application or résumé, and the candidate verbally agrees, courts have held that this is a valid waiver of the right to privacy, within the limited context that has already been described.

What's the best option for both prospective employee and prospective employer? Obviously, an express waiver, signed by the candidate, is best. With this type of waiver, there is no doubt about the intentions of both parties.

## HOW MANY REFERENCES SHOULD BE CHECKED?

My recommendation is to check three references. Why? During the last two decades that I've been in the reference-checking business, I've learned that checking only two references is not enough, and checking four or five becomes redundant and repetitious. More often than not, in those instances where one reference raves about the candidate and the second offers merely lukewarm comments, it is that third reference who can bring the picture into sharper focus. And, as I suggested earlier, the ideal set of references should include a superior, a peer, and a subordinate. The idea, of course, is to get an understanding of the candidate from various points of view. The way in which a job seeker is perceived by a former boss may be entirely different from that of a former subordinate—and that's an important difference to understand. Often it's the peer who can explain the incongruent perceptions.

45

Even if all the references turn out to be coworkers, the "rule of 3" is still the one to follow when reference checking. We have had some clients who wanted as many as a dozen references checked, especially for extremely important positions. If that's what the client wants, I would certainly do it, but I would never recommend it. If an accurate picture of the candidate can't be obtained after talking to three references, then it probably can't be obtained at all.

## What's the Difference between a Personal *Reference* and a Professional *Reference*?

A personal reference, by definition, is someone with whom the candidate has never worked. It's a sixth-grade teacher, or a scoutmaster, or somebody on a bowling team. From the standpoint of reference checking for employment purposes (even if you are just hiring someone to work on your home), personal references are a complete waste of time. What, after all, could a sixth-grade teacher have to say about a candidate's management style on the job? What would the local Brownie troop leader know about a candidate's career development needs? The answer: nothing! Employers, therefore, should insist that every candidate provide business or professional references. To be honest, the terms *business* and *professional*, within this context, mean about the same thing. They include people the candidate has worked with for at least six months, preferably longer.

I tend to think professional references are most appropriate for people working in the professions, such as lawyers, doctors, and the like. But regardless of whether they're called business or professional references, they're still people with whom the candidate has worked on a daily basis for a reasonable length of time.

It should be pointed out that many times the candidates will offer as references the names of people two or even three levels removed from their day-to-day work experience. While it may be nice that the president of the company has agreed to be a reference for the manager six levels below her, the president will probably know next to nothing about the actual job performance of the candidate. Again, references should be people with whom the candidate has actually worked—someone who would be able to comment on the type of questions outlined earlier. If there are too many layers of organizational structure between the candidate and the reference, you might as well be talking to the candidate's sixth-grade teacher.

The same holds true for landlords. A personal reference is someone from whom the prospective tenant has never rented before. If you're a landlord, the type of references you should request of prospective tenants is somewhat more limited. Nevertheless, insist on the names of at least three recent landlords or apartment managers and current contact information so you can easily reach all of them. I also think that in rental situations, it's a very good idea to at least verify current employment to avoid the obvious problem associated with being unable to collect the rent each month.

To help ensure that you, as landlord, are really talking to a former landlord, and not the prospective tenant's fishing buddy, there's a special little twist involved. My advice when placing the call is to say, "The reason I'm calling is your name was given for so-and-so as a reference—how are you acquainted with him/her?" The point is to determine the nature of the association between the prospective renter and the references *before* acknowledging that you're a landlord yourself. Then your questions should include some of the basics that the fishing buddy probably won't know, such as:

+ How long did he/she live in your complex? About from when to when?

+ What type of apartment was it? A townhouse? All on one floor? How many bedrooms? Where's the complex located? What's the exact address?

47

While you're asking these questions, you can have the prospective tenant's application right in front of you to cross-check the accuracy of the information provided by the reference. That's how you make sure the references provided are legitimate. The other thing you can do to ensure that legitimate references are being provided is to double-check the telephone number provided by the prospective tenant against the listing for the rental office in the telephone directory. These are just a few of the things you can do to make sure you're really talking to an appropriate reference.

## GETTING STARTED CHECKING REFERENCES

How should references be checked? In person? By mail? By telephone? Let's look at the pros and cons of each.

### *Mail*

Many employers still rely on one of the most archaic forms of reference checking—the mailed questionnaire. Why is it archaic? Much like a letter of recommendation, it is a one-way communication. How, for instance, does the prospective employer ask a follow-up question on a piece of paper? Suppose one of the questions is, "How would you rate the overall job performance of the candidate?" Now, suppose the written response is, "No one performed like she did." What does that response really mean? Is it laudatory or damning with faint praise? How could anyone possibly know?

Suppose the questionnaire asks the reference to describe the candidate's main strengths and the response comes back, "His skills doing A, B, and C were exceptional." What if, as the prospective employer, I want to know about the candidate's ability to handle skills D, E, and F? How do I find out about that? Obviously, I can't. That's why filling out a questionnaire is, for all intents and purposes, a waste of time. It's not possible to seek clarification on vague or incomplete responses; it's not even possible to verify who actually provided the information. As with letters of recommendation, countless employers who have agreed to serve as references will simply pass the questionnaire off to the person about whom the information is requested or ask the candidate to write his or her own letter of recommendation that the reference will then review (perhaps) and sign. How valid can that exercise ever be? That's why a mailed reference questionnaire is practically worthless.

On the other hand, if written letters of reference are the only documents a candidate has available, the logical thing to do is to simply ask permission of the candidate to make a follow-up call to the author of the letter to seek additional information not covered in the letter or to ask additional questions to further clarify statements that lack specificity or fall into the category of the "glittering generality."

## In Person

Not much space needs to be devoted to the value of going to see references. If money were no object, sitting down with references would be a very nice way to go about it. That could be a viable financial option if references happen to be located in the same town, and if they're willing to be interviewed in person. In addition, you could pick up on some of the more subtle signals during a face-to-face interview, such as body language or facial expression, but as a practical matter, most of the time going to see references is really not a viable option.

## Telephone

The best choice, therefore, is actually calling references and having a discussion with them about the candidate's past job performance. A conversation via telephone with a reference is, by definition, a two-way communication. If a response isn't clear, the prospective employer can ask for clarification or for more information. More importantly, the prospective employer or landlord (or whomever is placing the calls) can listen for things like tone of voice, inflection, nuance of meaning, and hesitations—all of which can prompt important follow-up questions.

The art of reference checking is two-fold. First, it is the art of careful listening. Second, it is the art of being able to ask follow-up questions. No one schooled in the art of reference checking would ever be satisfied, for example, with a response like "good." If I were talking with a reference and asked the question (which I have a thousand times) "How would you rate the overall quality of so-and-so's total job performance?" and I received a response like "good," my next question would be something like, "How would so-and-so compare to other people you've known doing the same type of work?" Or I might ask, "Good in what way?"

A more common response to that quality-of-performance question usually goes something like, "Oh, so-and-so was the best employee we ever had in that position!" Your follow-up question would be, "That's great! Could you give me some examples that might illustrate how so-and-so's performance was so exceptional?" If there is a long pause or if the reply is vague, you should wonder if so-and-so really was the best person ever to hold that position. You see the point. That's why conducting reference checks by phone is the best and most economical way to collect job performance information.

## What to Ask and How to Find Out
## What You Need to Know

The first step in this process is to understand that job performance is *not* job-specific. There are, in other words, commonalties of performance that apply to every job. For instance, I don't have to understand analytical spectroscopy to ask a reference how well the candidate performed that task. On the other hand, you'll likely have some job-specific questions you want asked or concerns about the candidate as the result of an interview. Even though there are standard questions that should always be asked, every reference call is unique to the extent that it is "tailored" to fit the concerns of the employer—either about the candidate or about the requirements of the job.

A basic list of questions, however, should include the following:

## General Information:

• How do you know the candidate?

• What were his/her responsibilities during the time you worked together?

## Performance Issues:

• How would you rate the overall quality of his/her job performance?

• How productive was the candidate?

• What were his/her main strengths on the job?

• How would you compare the candidate's overall performance to that of others you've worked with doing the same job?

• What do you think motivated him/her to want to do well on the job?

## Relating with Coworkers and Subordinates:

• How did he/she interact with others on the job?

• How was he/she perceived by others with whom he/she worked?

• How would you rate his/her communications skills?

◆ Did he/she supervise others? How many?

◆ How would you describe his/her management style?

**Growth Areas:**

◆ In what areas did he/she need to improve?

◆ What could he/she have done to achieve even better results on the job?

◆ What does he/she need to do in order to continue his/her professional growth?

**Closing Questions:**

◆ Why is he/she looking for other employment? Or, why did he/she leave?

◆ Would you hire him/her again? Or, is he/she eligible for rehire? Could he/she have stayed if he/she had wanted to?

◆ And, finally, is there anything else you'd like to add about his/her job performance that I haven't already asked?

Clearly, this is not an all-encompassing list of questions, but it should give some idea of how a structured reference interview should go. Each one of the questions listed can be accompanied by follow-up questions that seek amplification, illustration, and clarification of the initial response—that's where reference checking becomes an art. Supplemental questions that are job-specific or candidate-specific should be asked at the end of the more general job-performance-based questions. More sample questions are available in the Appendix.

## What Not to Ask!

Put in the most simple terms, if the question has nothing to do with job performance, don't ask it. Note that all the questions outlined previously relate specifically to job performance. There are, however, other questions that should never, never be asked. They include questions about age, race, sex, religion, national origin, medical, marital status, or sexual orientation. All of these categories are protected by federal law in the sense that basing an employment decision on any of them could easily cause an employer to find him- or herself in a federal discrimination lawsuit. As a simple rule of thumb, if it's personal information that has nothing to do with past job performance or job performance potential, or with the requirements of the job to be done, don't ask it! On a more practical level, why would any employer need to know, for instance, where somebody goes to church? What possible bearing could that have on job performance? Common sense, again, is always a factor in the equation about what to ask and not ask.

But, you reply, shouldn't my church know the religious affiliation of the candidate we're considering for our office secretary? No. You don't *need* to know that to make an intelligent employment decision. The goal is still the same—hiring the best person for the job to be done. It is *not* appropriate to eliminate otherwise-qualified candidates for employment on the basis of religion, *unless* part of the job description requires being well-versed in the church's dogma, procedures, or traditions as essential to the religious mission of the institution.

Here's one other exception to the nondiscrimination laws: Suppose you and your spouse want to hire a child care provider. Are you also bound by the same antidiscrimination laws we have been discussing? No. Why not? Because federal civil rights laws only apply to employers of 15 people or more. State civil rights laws will vary somewhat, depending on the state. However, no employer, not even our couple just looking for a child care provider, can discriminate on the basis of race. There is a federal law, the 1866 Civil Rights Act, that prohibits "color" discrimination in the making of contracts.

There will always be gray areas when we start talking about unusual situations like the two just described, but as a general rule, employment decisions should not be based on any factor except job performance.

## HOW TO GET BEYOND THE BASICS

Getting beyond the basics is where the art of reference checking comes into play. Getting beyond the basics requires, more than anything else, common sense. Conducting a reference interview should be a conversation, just like one you'd have with someone about which car dealer he likes and why. Earlier in this chapter, I gave you a list of questions to ask references. They represent the framework around which to structure your conversation. Each of those questions can elicit a brief or a detailed response. It's not the detailed responses about which you need to worry; you'll get plenty of information you can use. It's the one-word responses that require your common sense. If, for instance, you ask about the overall quality of the candidate's job performance and the response is nothing more than "good," you need to be prepared to follow-up with a question like, "Where would you rate 'good' on, say, a scale of 1 to 10?" Or if you ask the reference about areas of improvement and the response is something like, "He/she did every aspect of the job very well," you have to be prepared to counter with, "That's great to hear, but surely there was some area where he/she could improve. None of us is perfect, after all." It's within the context of the follow-up question that the details lie. The keys are being good at listening—really listening to what the reference has to say—and thinking about what you really want to know and being politely persistent. If you look over the list of recommended questions, you'll notice that several of them come at the same qualities from different directions. So, even if you're worried about how insightful you can be, by the time you've talked to three references, you should have a very good overall picture of not only how well the person has performed, but also how that performance matches the requirements of the job to be filled, as well as the areas in which improvement is needed.

Real reference checking has more to do with finding out about a potential employee's "soft skills," such as the ability to work productively with others or to function as a member of a team, than it does with technical expertise. While technical expertise is important, study after study proves that interpersonal skills, broadly defined, are the most important. Why? Because very few jobs can be done successfully in a vacuum. Ninety-nine percent of all jobs require interaction with others, at least some of the time. To put it another way, people seldom get into arguments with machines. Ordinarily, disputes are limited to people interacting with other people. Being able to get along with others in a work setting, therefore, is vital at a very fundamental level. People can be taught to operate the widget machine; it's quite another thing to have the skill to teach people how to work effectively with others.

## WHO SHOULD MAKE THE PHONE CALL

Reference checking should be performed by the same person who is doing the interview, or at least someone involved in the hiring process. Far too often, the task of checking references is delegated to a clerical person who has no training, and the result is that follow-up questions aren't asked and many areas of concern are glossed over lightly. If you are doing the interviewing, you know what the job requires, what challenges the person hired must face, what the personalities on your team are, and so on. That makes you the best person for knowing the specific follow-up questions to ask.

## VERIFY ALL DEGREES AND LICENSES

This is a step that many people overlook, and it's one of the easiest parts of the selection process. Not too long ago Ed Bradley did a segment on *60 Minutes* called "Unmasked." Here's what he said:

> "The next time you or someone you know checks into a hospital to have major surgery, there's a good chance the people behind the surgical masks taking part in the operation will not have a medical license. Yet that won't stop these 'surgical assistants,' as they're called, from doing many of the same things that a licensed surgeon does in millions of complex operations each year . . . We found that in a lot of hospitals, there's little or no checking of their credentials. And what's more, some of them actually tell patients that they are doctors, and bill them at doctors' rates, when in fact they have never had a license to practice medicine."

Why aren't they verifying medical licenses? According to *60 Minutes*, surgeons and hospital administrators say they're too busy.

The truth of the matter is, verifying any type of license—from the one required to practice medicine to the one required to fly a plane—is nothing more than a quick phone call away. For physicians, there is a state licensing board that can—and will—verify whether or not an individual is licensed to practice medicine in that state. The same is true for lawyers, teachers, dentists, realtors, pilots, beauticians, plumbers, electricians, and any other occupation that requires licensing. All that's required is calling the issuing agency and asking if so-and-so has a currently valid license!

Checking academic credentials is just as easy. All it requires is a quick call to the registrar's office of the college or university from which the degree is claimed. The way to ask the question is merely to say something like, "Can you verify for me that so-and-so earned a B.S. degree in whatever from your school in such-and-such year?" That's all there is to it. For more on checking degrees and licenses, including tricks of the trade for getting more information, see Chapter 7, "Ancillary Checks: How to Supplement Your Research." One more point, the most practical thing to do is only verify the highest degree claimed. Here's why: You can't earn a master's degree unless you've earned a bachelor's degree first. So checking the highest degree claimed is the most sensible thing to do.

## REFERENCE-CHECKING TIPS

To summarize the main lessons from this chapter, there are a few things that every hiring manager should remember:

- Always have every candidate sign a comprehensive waiver.

- Check at least three references.

- Insist on specific categories of references.

- Confine all questions to job performance.

- Avoid personal references.

- Verify all degrees and licenses.

- Check references by telephone.

- Ask open-ended questions. For example, ask "How would you describe so-and-so's management style?" and not "Was so-and-so an effective hands-on manager?"

- Never ask questions about personal matters in the protected categories we outlined. They don't have anything to do with job performance, and you could easily find yourself in a discrimination lawsuit.

# CHAPTER 5

# MAXIMIZING THE VALUE OF WHAT YOU LEARN

Good reference checking, as we've discussed it thus far, accomplishes one primary objective: It helps ensure that you're hiring the right person for the job—the first time. But there's so much more to it. Let's discuss the wider-ranging benefits that come from true reference checking so that you, the prospective employer, can take full advantage of *all* of them.

There really is a triple benefit that comes from job performance-based reference checking, and we'll talk about each benefit in this chapter. So, the goal of this chapter is to help you maximize the value of information derived from a thorough reference check.

## EVALUATING HOW WELL THE CANDIDATE HAS PERFORMED IN THE PAST

Throughout this book we've focused on the key role past job performance (or previous rental experience) plays in predicting future job performance (or tenant behavior). In fact, it's the *best* indication available to you. Disregarding (for the moment) the specific demands

of the position you need to fill, a careful analysis of past job performance is the first of your "triple hit" benefits that come from the
exercise. Remember how illuminating this information can be upon
skilled analysis? We've talked about the importance of viewing the
candidate's performance *over time* and from *different points of
view*. You'll recall the two primary reasons for doing that are (1) to
look for *consistency* among the comments made by references
about various aspects of the candidate's overall performance and
(2) to look for *patterns of career growth, professional development*,
plus areas of performance that have *changed* as the candidate's
career has unfolded.

The key to this information is to ask "standard" questions of every
reference (see Appendix A). The reason for asking these standard
questions is that, no matter what the job or occupation, the answers
are useful across the board. For example, asking, "What do you think
so-and-so's main strength is/was on the job?" would be an appropriate and important question that applies to every candidate for
employment, from accountant to church organist to zoologist. In
much the same way, a question like "What could so-and-so have
done to have gotten even better results on the job?" is pertinent to the
same range of occupations. In other words, it doesn't matter what
the job is; questions like the two cited previously have universal
worthiness as indicators of past job performance.

So, the evaluation of past job performance is critical to establishing a "base line," if you will, that will tell if the fundamentals
you're looking for are basically there. When taking a backward
glance at job performance, what we're really interested in is confirmation and validation of fundamental job behaviors, skill sets, and
core competencies across time and from a variety of perspectives.
Confirmation of things like job responsibilities is important, but if
you look closely, you'll discover that at least half of the standard

questions listed in Appendix A have more to do with "soft" skills than they do with how well the candidate could design, build, or operate any particular machine. Furthermore, you'll notice these are questions that relate to professional demeanor, motivation, quality of performance, productivity, interaction with others, communication skills, and management style. Put in simpler terms, it doesn't matter nearly as much what the candidate did, as it does how well it was done and how effective he or she was in relation to and in conjunction with others.

If the candidate, in the broader sense, could get the job done through working well with people—whatever the job happened to be—it is more likely than not he or she will continue to be able to accomplish future tasks using the same approach. And you'll be able to confirm this through the process of talking with multiple references.

Talking to *multiple* references . . . that's really the key to the evaluation, confirmation, and validation of past job performance. Since the same basic questions are asked of all references, cross-comparison not only becomes possible, but it also becomes an essential part of the process. That's why it's so important to make sure the questions listed in Appendix A are asked the same way and in the same order during each conversation with each reference. Note that the questions do not fall in random order but are sequentially arranged to go from the very general and objective to the very specific and subjective. Carefully structured questions like these allow you, the person talking with references, to build some rapport, trust, and camaraderie early on in the conversation. As you become more probing, the more subjective the questions become. And because the references will have been put at ease, the more comfortable they'll feel responding to your questions. (What it really boils down to is having a cordial, yet structured *conversation* about the candidate. This should be your goal with every reference.) The worst thing that can happen is for you to sound stiff, mechanical, or bored with the exercise. The more enthusiasm, curiosity, and polish you bring to the exercise, the more successful you will be putting references at ease. This is one of the most important parts of the process—*if* you want to get solid, candid, and thoughtful job performance information about the candidate.

The same approach holds true when dealing with multiple candidates being considered for the same position. Suppose you've narrowed down your list of prospective candidates to the top three. Furthermore, based on their credentials and interviewing skills, all three appear to be more-or-less equally qualified. You can expect differences (perhaps not *major* differences, but at least some differences) to emerge when references are called. So it is especially important to pose the same questions, in the same way, and in the same sequence to each candidate.

If nothing else is done except the formal evaluation of past job performance, you, as the person responsible for the hiring decision, will be able to discover a qualitative distinction among your top candidates. The chances of all three candidates in our theoretical example still being equal following a thorough reference check is next to impossible.

The point that needs to be kept in mind throughout the process is that reference checking is not an attempt to uncover the fraud or the liar—although that does happen occasionally. The object of the exercise is to identify the candidate who has performed well consistently, has grown in his or her professional career, and has demonstrated that he or she has the basic skill sets, both technical and interactional, to remain in contention for the position to be filled.

## COMPARING PAST JOB PERFORMANCE WITH THE REQUIREMENTS OF THE JOB

This concerns the second benefit of careful reference checking. First of all, everyone needs to understand that no two jobs are ever exactly alike. The title of the position may be the same, and the responsibilities may be the same, but no two companies operate in exactly the same way. Even though two job descriptions may be exactly alike, the reality is that there will be slight differences between jobs, because, if for no other reason, different people and personalities are involved. Therefore, the notion that different organizations have different corporate cultures is clearly true.

You, as the person responsible for making hiring decisions, need to understand the requirements of the job to be filled at two different levels of cognition. First, there is the formal job description that officially outlines the exact parameters of the job. Second is the practical job description, which probably isn't written down anywhere, but defines the way the job really works within the framework of the other people, politics, and peculiarities within the organization.

For instance, if you're hiring a functional manager, the management style you require may be totally influenced by the characteristics of the people being managed. If, for example, the group is composed of senior-level employees who've been with the company for long periods of time, the new manager's approach will be totally different than if the group is composed of younger, less experienced employees. You, as the hiring manager, need to know that, because it will have a direct bearing on the requirements of the position. This may not be chiseled in stone anywhere, or stated in formal terms, but it makes sense in everyday, real-world terms.

Or, suppose you have a very independent group of people which requires a very hands-on manager who has the training and experience to mold them into a smooth-running and efficient team. Now suppose that when you start asking references about your top candidate's management style, all of them say that he or she delegates responsibility very effectively and prefers a hands-off style—that person may not be right for the job. There's nothing inherently wrong with this candidate; it may be nothing more than his or her management style not being right for this particular position.

Another example is when the person who held a position in the past created a situation or an atmosphere within the organization that needs to be "corrected." It might be an internal problem—say, interdepartmental friction—or it might concern external relations with the general public or with the company's customer base. In any case, the new candidate for the job faces (often) unspoken challenges that need to be taken into consideration by the person doing the hiring.

One more example: Suppose you're hiring a contractor to, let's say, add a family room to your home. The requirements of the job may be very straightforward in terms of things like dimensions, the pitch of the roof, and the types of materials to be used. If you know, however, that you or a spouse have particular expectations with regard to things like attention to detail, staying precisely within budget, and the careful selection of things like light fixtures, crown molding, or whatever, you'll want to ask questions of the prospective contractor's references that address your concerns. Some contractors, obviously, take more pride in their work than others, so that's definitely something about which you'll want to ask with some specificity.

So, knowing the requirements of the job, both formal and informal, is critical in the employee selection process.

Now, because every job varies slightly, there probably will be special concerns that you, as the hiring manager, will want to build into your standard list of questions. Let's refer back to the example involving the mature, long-tenured employees. Knowing that a new employee will face a different set of management challenges than would be presented by the younger group still in the process of growing into their jobs, you may well want to tailor or supplement the reference interview to address this particular concern. In this instance, it would be entirely appropriate to say to references—toward the end of the conversation—something like, "The group that so-and-so will be managing has been with the company for a considerable length of time and are pretty set in their ways. How do you think so-and-so will do trying to initiate change within that sort of group?" Clearly, that *specific* question is not to be found in Appendix A, but it is of equal importance in terms of making a good hiring decision.

Let's look at this from yet another point of view. Suppose you've interviewed a licensed home health care worker who, during the interview, gave you the impression that he might be short-tempered.

How can you check that out? Do exactly the same thing when talking to references: Simply add a question to the standard list. Again, toward the end of the conversation, you might ask, "You know, I sort of picked up during my interview with so-and-so that he might be a little short-tempered at times. What do you think about that?" Or, "How does so-and-so handle stressful situations?" Or, "How would you describe so-and-so's general temperament?" Wait to ask specific questions like this until after asking the general question about the candidate's personality and attitude on the job (Question 7 in Appendix A).

There's one more important way to address an issue like this. Let's say that the interview went well, and you have no reason to believe the candidate has any kind of problem with his temper. (Here's where the art of reference checking comes in.) Suppose you are asking a reference to describe the candidate's personality or attitude on the job, and the reference starts to equivocate a little with you, saying something like, "Well, so-and-so can sometimes be pretty demanding." Here's precisely the point at which you should ask, "Oh, really? In what way"? Or if the reference overtly suggests that the candidate can be short-tempered, you should ask something like, "Could you tell me a little more about that. Short-tempered how?"

Do you see? The reference-checking process requires being able to pick up on subtle clues during interviews that relate to work behaviors. These insights can translate into performance-specific follow-up questions. That means developing critical listening skills— listening for things like hesitations, changes in tone of voice or inflection, and nuances of meaning. When you notice these things happening, ask the reference for clarification.

Finally, using our short-tempered candidate example once more, regardless of *how* you get the impression the candidate might be short-tempered, you need to address that possibility with *all three* references to either confirm or refute the suspicion to your satisfaction.

In conclusion, it's always important to know the requirements of the job, the dynamics of the work environment, and the less obvious characteristics of the candidate to enable you to supplement your basic list of questions. These additional questions can help you make sure the candidate's past job performance, no matter how good it sounded during the job interview, fits the particular requirements of the position you need to fill.

## CREATING A CAREER DEVELOPMENT PROGRAM BASED ON REFERENCE CHECKS

The third benefit of reference checking is using the results to come up with a career development plan for the candidate once he or she is hired. This is one of the most valuable, but often overlooked, benefits of careful reference checking.

One of the key questions to ask any reference is this: "What do you think the candidate needs to really continue his/her professional growth or career development?" This is the question that will help enable you to build a career plan for this individual to increase his or her value to the organization, either in the near-term or over the long haul.

The first thing to do, of course, is to realize that every candidate, no matter how accomplished or skilled, can improve. None of us is perfect. There will always be things we can do to gain more knowledge or experience, become more adept at working with others, or improve our performance of a million other job-related skills. The one constant is the potential to become more than we are in our individual careers. Once that truism is internalized, then you have opened the door to useful insight as to how a candidate can become more valuable to the organization.

The answer to the question just cited (Question 18 in Appendix A) is intentionally positioned where it is on the list because it is essentially subjective in nature and calls for an opinion—perhaps based on solid fact—from references.

To illustrate the point, I recall doing a reference report on a candidate who was being considered for a position as a senior design engineer. Part of the requirements of the job included being able to make effective presentations to top management and also to prospective clients. In short, all three references consistently described the candidate as being very professional, thoroughly trained, and having solid experience in a design engineering position. However, when I asked what the candidate needed to do to continue his professional growth, two of the three said emphatically that he needed to polish his presentation skills because he just wasn't a very convincing or effective speaker. The third reference didn't even need that much prompting. When I asked if there were any areas in which the candidate needed to improve, she immediately cited his presentation skills!

When I got to the question about career growth, I modified it by saying, "Is there anything *else* you think the candidate needs to continue his career growth?"

The response was, "No, just improvement in his presentation skills."

So, did a lack of skill in making presentations knock this candidate out of further consideration for employment? Absolutely not! The prospective employer was impressed enough with the other aspects of his past job performance that he was hired anyway. But the company almost immediately got him enrolled in a public-speaking course at an area college. After one semester, not only did the individual significantly improve his speaking skills, but he also voluntarily enrolled in another speaking course to further enhance his ability to make forceful and effective presentations. Armed with the knowledge of what the candidate needed to advance his career and meet the requirements of the job, the question must be asked, "Did the reference report enable the employer to increase the candidate's value to the organization?" The answer? Yes, without question. I would also suggest that without checking references, there was no other way the prospective employer could have garnered that information and avoided what could have been a job mismatch. Clearly, the candidate would not have admitted during his job interview, "Oh, and by the way, my presentation skills stink."

Another example that illustrates the point is the client we had some time ago who wanted to hire a sales manager. They had identified their top choice and had us prepare a reference report. The job required industry-specific product knowledge of an unusually high degree because of the highly technical nature of the product. The job also called for excellent interpersonal skills. The candidate had the required product knowledge and people skills, but he had never managed the time and activities of others. Again, the company hired him and put him into a crash course in sales management. To give the candidate time to develop the necessary managerial skills, he was initially hired as a salesperson. This gave him time to become familiar with intricacies of the product line and learn more about the client base. Within six months, the candidate had acquired both theoretical and managerial knowledge, but in his spare time, the company also had him do job-shadowing of another sales manager. Then he was promoted to the sales manager's position. In this instance, no one had asked the candidate if he had any supervisory experience, because they were so impressed with his existing product knowledge and interpersonal skills. But it was the reference report that gave the employer the information needed to turn what could have been a hiring mistake into a valuable addition to their managerial team.

In this chapter we discussed how to get the most value from the information you learn in a reference check and have seen that there are three separate and distinct benefits to careful job-performance-based reference checking:

+ You get a thorough evaluation of how well the candidate has performed in the past.

+ You learn how that performance fits the requirements of the job.

+ Performance-based reference checking provides a basis for developing a career growth plan to enhance the employee's value to the employer—either in the short run or over time.

Reference checking, then, is more than just a one-dimensional exercise. It can provide anyone who employs people with extraordinary insights, which cannot really be obtained in any other way. These are insights not only into how to compare past performance to the particular requirements of a job, but also into bringing added value to the employee through individually tailored career growth.

# CHAPTER 6

# COMMON PROBLEMS AND HOW TO HANDLE THEM

With each reference you check, you'll likely encounter some responses, or even lack of responses, to which you'll need to know how to respond. For example, how can you be sure the answers to your questions are honest? What if the candidate is just out of college? What if he or she has a criminal record? In this chapter, you'll learn how to respond to these and many more potential problems.

## HOW DO I DETERMINE IF A REFERENCE IS RELIABLE?

One of the common problems people face when checking someone's references is trying to determine the reliability of the comments. There are, however, two sides to this particular coin. On one side is the person seeking employment; on the other, the person doing the hiring. It is only natural to expect job seekers to provide references they believe will only say good things about them. That expectation leads many people, in business and elsewhere, to think that checking those given references is just a waste of time. "If I'm just talking to references provided by the job seeker," the thinking goes, "aren't those people simply going to say how great the candidate is, no matter what? I need objective information, not an overinflated assessment that's unreasonably biased."

The point those people are missing is that the person doing the hiring has far more control than they may realize. As we've discussed before, the responsibility to provide meaningful references should fall on the job seeker. But identifying the *type* of references required by the prospective employer is the responsibility of the employer or the person doing the hiring. Tell the candidate what you want! This is no "power trip" on your part; you're really helping the genuinely qualified candidate to make a more favorable impression on you (or the hiring committee you represent). This is basic standard HR operating procedure in professional employment situations. Once you understand that, and clearly relate your requirements to the candidate, the responsibility shifts to the candidate to come up with references who fit your need for information.

This principle holds true in every hiring situation, regardless. It doesn't matter if you're looking for a new minister for your church, someone to run the company day care center or the public library, or someone to come in every week and help with the housework at home. You can and should specify the type of references to be supplied.

We've already talked about what a waste of time personal references are. Everyone involved in hiring should insist on being given the names of people with whom the job seeker has *actually worked.* No best friends, no former scoutmasters, no favorite teachers from school days, no college roommates.

Even if this unwritten rule is followed to the letter, how can you be sure the comments made by given references are reliable? Is it tempting for a job seeker to try and pass off a relative or close friend as a work-related reference? You bet. There are several things employers can and should do to increase the likelihood of receiving honest responses to job performance questions:

- Always ask the job seeker to provide a résumé that contains a complete work history, including dates of employment for every job held.

- Also, ask that the candidate provide the name of the person to whom the candidate directly reported. Do this regardless of whether it was the chair of the church board, the school principal, a production line supervisor, or the name of the landlord who collected the rent.

- Employers should always require candidates for employment to fill out a formal job application that asks for the same information. One way or another, then, whether it's on the résumé, or the job application, even if you have to ask for it during the initial interview, you'll get a description of the tasks for which the job seeker was responsible at each position held.

If the list of references doesn't include at least one of the people to whom the candidate reported, a red flag should go up in the prospective employer's mind. Some job seekers will contend, legitimately, that they didn't list a previous supervisor as a reference because the two of them didn't get along. That's understandable. None of us gets along with everybody all of the time. But throughout an individual's entire work history, there has to be at least one supervisor who can be a reference. If that isn't possible, then it's best to look for another person for the job. If it's true the candidate has never gotten along with *any* supervisor *ever*, that should be a major red flag.

## Interviewing Techniques for Determining Reliability

To verify the reliability of a reference, first establish the nature of the association between the candidate and the previous employer. One of the best ways to avoid talking to Uncle Harry, who's trying to do his favorite nephew a favor by pretending to be a former boss, is by asking relationship questions at the beginning of the interview. Here's how the dialogue might go:

Begin by identifying yourself. "Hi, I'm so-and-so and I'm with (*name of organization, company, school, hospital, whatever*). We're considering (*name*) for a position with our organization and he/she gave your name as a reference. I was wondering if we could chat about him/her for a few minutes."

It's conceivable the person on the phone legitimately cannot spare several minutes at that particular time to discuss the candidate. If that's the case, kindly offer to call back at a more convenient time and follow through accordingly. Once you reconnect, be certain to not reveal the title or type of position to be filled and continue with something like this: "Let me begin by asking you, how are you acquainted with (*name*)?" No matter what the response to that question is, your next question should be, "How long did the two of you work together?" Or, "How long were you directly associated with (*name*)?"

*Note:* At this point, there should be a direct correlation between those two questions and the job described or the candidate's résumé or the job application in your hands. If the information doesn't match, you have two choices: (1) ask the reference to explain the discrepancy or (2) ask one or two questions, such as "Why did so-and-so leave?" and "How would you rate his/her performance?" and then politely end the conversation. The lack of correlation, in other words, should be a huge red flag because *someone* isn't being completely honest.

The next thing to do is to confirm the identity of the reference by asking where he or she is currently employed. Ask what his or her job title is, as well. It could be the same place where the reference and the candidate knew each other, but it could be somewhere entirely different if the reference has moved on to another job. *Note:* The point here is to verify the identity of the reference by confirming his or her place of employment and job title.

Next, ask the reference to describe the candidate's responsibilities on the job during the time they worked together. This is a crucial question, and more often then not, it will reveal whether or not you're really talking to a legitimate reference. Why? Because even if good old Uncle Harry was coached on where the candidate worked and how long he was there, it is unlikely he'll know in any detail exactly what tasks were being performed. So, the dialogue might continue in a vein such as this: "So you and (*name*) worked together for two years and he reported to you all that time. Fine. What, then, were his primary responsibilities on the job? In other words, what was he being paid to do?"

If you get a vague response like, "Oh, he handled lots of different projects," the follow-up question would then be something like, "Could you give me some specific examples of a couple of projects he handled?"

Poor Uncle Harry will be lost by this point. And you both will know it. I would submit there is no way a reference could successfully fake answers to such questions. You will have the candidate's version of the facts right in front of you—the job title, the dates of employment, the place of employment, and the responsibilities carried out. If none of the information matches, it's high time to be more than a little suspicious.

This, initially, is a good way to determine if references are not only legitimate, but also reliable. Remember, these types of questions apply across the board, regardless of the occupational category. Frankly, where most fake references fall apart is on the "How are you acquainted with (*name*)?" question. Most pretend references will fumble and say something like, "Oh, we've been friends for years," which should lead you to ask questions like those just mentioned: "Have you ever worked together?" "In what capacity?" "About how long?" "Where?"

## WHAT ABOUT TRULY LEGITIMATE REFERENCES? HOW DO YOU KNOW THEY'RE GIVING YOU HONEST ANSWERS?

Let's say the reference provided passes all the tests of legitimacy. Can you totally rely on whatever the reference has to say about the candidate? Again, the types of questions you ask make all the difference. For instance, a very good question is, "How would you rate the overall quality of (*name*)'s job performance?" If the answer comes back as something like, "Charlie was the best employee we ever had," the next question should logically be, "Well, that's great; could you give me some examples that illustrate how Charlie's performance was so exceptional?" If the reference can't think of any examples to make the point, some doubt would have to be cast on how great Charlie's performance really was.

Here's another way to measure honesty. Suppose you need to hire a hands-on manager who can get out there, roll up her sleeves, bring together a group of people who are all flying around in different directions and turn them into a smoothly running team. Then, the question to ask references would not be, "Is Mary a hands-on manager?" Instead, it would be, "How would you describe Mary's management style?" There is no way a reference will be able to second-guess the type of manager you're looking for based on that question. Suppose, after talking to three references, they've all essentially told you Mary is really great at delegating responsibility to subordinates and then letting them complete tasks on their own. That could mean Mary's really not right for the job. She may be a great person, but she's not the one for the job that needs to be done. *Note:* This example is precisely why it's never satisfactory to talk to only one reference, and why I recommend talking to three. The object of the exercise is consistency among the comments. That's how to ensure you're getting honest information about the candidate.

## WHAT IF YOU FEEL A REFERENCE IS TRYING TO SABOTAGE A GREAT CANDIDATE?

This sort of thing won't happen very often if the responsibility of providing references is placed on the candidate. Why would anyone ever ask a coworker he or she didn't really trust to serve as a reference? It makes no sense to do that. Nevertheless, it does occasionally happen, and that's another reason why you should check at least three references. In my 20-plus years in the reference-checking business, I've never, ever seen a case where all three references were trying to sabotage a good candidate. If two of the references rave about the candidate's overall job performance and one essentially says the candidate was a bum, common sense would tell you that something might be amiss.

The solution? Simply ask the candidate to provide a couple of additional references. Then, hopefully, the opportunity will come to casually ask one of those new references why so-and-so's comments were so negative. While that may not always be possible, additional confirmation about the candidate's performance—one way or the other—should be forthcoming from the additional references. The other thing you can consider doing after references have been contacted is to ask the candidate about the sort of working relationship he or she had with the reference who made the negative comments. That should provide additional insight, if any is needed, into why the negative comments were made.

## HOW CAN I DEAL WITH A "NO COMMENT" POLICY?

This is one of the most perplexing problems faced by people responsible for hiring other people, and it is a situation found not so much outside the corporate world, but within it. Many companies, by policy, place restrictions on what their employees can say about a former employee. Typically, they are instructed to refer all calls to HR, which, of course, defeats the whole purpose of providing references. How could anyone in an HR office know anything about the former employee's management style? They can't; and in most cases, all they will do is confirm employment dates and possibly a job title. How much help is that? This is precisely why the burden of providing references *who will talk* should be placed on the candidate.

Explain to the candidate when you're discussing what types of references you require that this kind of policy is sometimes in place. But the onus is on them to supply references who will *not* be constrained by any such policy. In other words, tell the candidate to ask around ahead of time. Neither the candidate nor you, the prospective employer, can benefit in any way from a reference who is forced into silence by some kind of corporate gag order.

For example, consider this scenario: Suppose you ask the candidate to provide appropriate references, and you're supplied with the name of a recent supervisor that you have been given express permission to call. (You've made the dangerous assumption that the candidate has already asked that person to serve as a reference.) You make the call only to be told by the supervisor that their company policy forbids him or her from saying anything about your candidate. Could that be a red flag or someone just following company policy? It doesn't matter. Regardless of the reason the person won't or can't talk, you will not get the information you need to make the best employment decision possible. What to do? Go right back to the candidate and tell him or her to either convince that reference to talk to you or find an appropriate substitute who will. Now, if none of the candidate's references agree to talk to you, then that should be a major red flag, especially if the candidate provided them. Of course, the best way to avoid this whole scenario is to clear the air in the first place (when discussing what types of references you require). Mention that sometimes the subject is touchy with some companies, but breaking through the silence barrier is important if the person wants to be seriously considered for the job.

Practically speaking, the reality of the situation is that people who have worked together for any length of time will usually talk to a prospective employer—in spite of company policy.

## How Can You Help a Cooperative Candidate Supply "Talking" References?

From the standpoint of the person doing the hiring, here are some useful suggestions to help the candidate come up with references who will talk:

- Find out if the reference would be willing to accept a call at home, or over the weekend, instead of at the office.

- Remind the reference that he or she isn't being asked to speak on behalf of the company, but only to provide honestly held opinions or to state documented facts.

- Since references shoud include people with whom the candidate has worked within the past five to seven years, it's entirely possible to find excellent references among people who've recently retired, taken jobs with other employers, or moved to other locations within the organization.

## WHAT IF THE CANDIDATE DOESN'T WANT THE CURRENT EMPLOYER TO KNOW HE OR SHE IS LOOKING FOR A JOB?

There are instances where a long-term employee decides to make a career move. The problem stems from the employee not wanting his or her current employer to know anything about these plans. How is that person supposed to come up with references that will be suitable without giving away the impending career change? This is a difficult problem, but not one that is unsolvable.

Reread the third point at the end of the last section. Excellent references can come from the ranks of those who have retired, recently changed jobs, or moved within the employing organization. But those aren't the only possibilities—especially if the prospective employer wants to talk to current coworkers, superiors, and subordinates.

Consider the fact that the candidate is a long-term employee of many years. During that time it is more than likely close personal friendships will have been developed among several people with whom the prospective candidate has worked. In other words, there will be people who can safely be asked to serve as references and not disclose it to anyone within the organization. From the candidate's perspective, it amounts to knowing whom you can trust. Anyone with 10 or more years of service to an organization shouldn't have trouble finding those kinds of friends/references. People who have worked together for years and become friends in the process should be able to ask each other for favors like this. And among long-time friends, a request for confidentiality most likely will be respected.

From the prospective employer's point of view, a candidate's request not to contact a current employer should always be respected. If, for some reason, the candidate isn't the right person for the job, that person's current employment should never be jeopardized. Never violate a unilateral request not to contact a candidate's current employer. But the solution to the problem of providing references remains the same: The responsibility is on the candidate to come up with the type of references you want, regardless of whether or not the candidate is a long-term employee. It may take some creativity, but it can be done. If it can't, look for someone else to fill the job.

## WHAT IF THE JOB SEEKER IS RIGHT OUT OF SCHOOL AND NEVER REALLY WORKED?

Another common problem is dealing with a young person just out of school who has never really worked. Well, it can easily be done, but the *focus* of the exercise is just a little different. Instead of talking about past job performance, the emphasis shifts toward job performance *potential*, but not completely.

First let's talk about the young person just out of college who has never had a professional job. There are several ideal sources for references: a former major professor, a faculty advisor, a club or organization sponsor, someone with whom the student worked as part of a campus or community activity, someone for whom the student worked as an intern or even someone for whom the student worked during a summer job. The way the focus shifts is how some of the questions are asked; part of them go from being past tense to future tense. For instance, instead of asking, "How *did* so-and-so get along with others?" the question becomes, "How do you think so-and-so *will* get along with others in a work setting?" A lot of the standard reference-checking questions remain the same, however. Asking about job performance as a student suggests things like class participation, attendance, getting work in on time, and, to be candid, academic ability. It should be noted, however, that the same professor

81

can also be asked, as a follow-up question, for his or her opinion on how the student *will* perform in a specific position. So for college students with little or no work experience, solid reference information can be obtained, with just a slight shift in focus.

For the young person who didn't attend college and who has only minimal work experience, reference checking can still be done—and in essentially the same way. Adequate references can include a high school counselor, coach, principal, or teacher. Employers for whom the young person has worked during the summer or on a part-time basis during the school year will also work. For employers, the approach is the same as with any references. For school-related references, again, there is a slight shift in focus in terms of asking not only about attendance, participation, and so forth, but also asking them to speculate a little about how, based on their assessment of the former student, he or she is *likely* to perform on the job.

On balance, the speculative nature of the reference-checking exercise is slightly different, but the adequacy of the information, since most young people aren't being considered for senior-level positions anyway, should be more than sufficient to make good, informed employment decisions.

## WHAT IF THE CANDIDATE WAS FIRED FROM THE LAST JOB?

If your job is to ensure that the best candidates possible are being hired, one of the things you'll want to know is why the candidate left his or her last place of employment (assuming the candidate is currently unemployed). How do you obtain this information?

At the end of every reference call, you should ask one or all of the following questions:

+ Do you know why so-and-so is currently looking for other employment?

♦ Would you hire him/her again? If so, what type of position do you think he/she would be best suited for?

♦ Could so-and-so have stayed with (*previous employer*) if he/she had wanted to?

♦ Is so-and-so eligible for rehire, as far as you know?

♦ What were the circumstances surrounding so-and-so's departure from (*previous employer*)?

Compare the responses to these questions to the stated reasons for leaving provided on the job application. Some of the common ways job seekers try to avoid using the word *fired* on a job application is to use euphemisms like "by mutual agreement," or "reduction in labor force," or "company reorganization." While any of these responses could be absolutely valid, sometimes these kinds of phrases are used as weasel words to avoid saying he or she was fired. That's why it's so important to ask multiple references why the candidate left. Sometimes it's possible to ask this question in multiple ways (like the questions listed previously) in order to get to the bottom of what really happened. Lying on a *résumé* is, or at least should be, one of the quickest disqualifiers for further consideration for employment.

From the job seeker's standpoint, using the phrase "termination—will explain" is probably the best thing to do. It is possible for people to lose their jobs for reasons that should not ruin their careers, and they should be given an opportunity to explain it. The prospective employer should also be given the opportunity to verify it, as well.

## WHAT IF THE CANDIDATE HAS A CRIMINAL RECORD?

Very few candidates will admit on a job application or *résumé* that they've been convicted of anything other than a minor traffic violation. Rightly or wrongly, they believe that admitting a criminal

record is a sure disqualifier from further consideration for employment. As a practical matter, they're generally right. But suppose you
do a court check (which we will talk about in much greater detail in
Chapter 7) and discover that the candidate has, in fact, a criminal
record. You have to consider several things:

+ How long ago was the conviction and for what? Should a drunk-
  driving conviction a decade ago preclude someone from ever
  gaining employment? Probably not.
+ Has there been more than one conviction within the recent past,
  and for what?
+ Were the convictions misdemeanors or felonies?
+ Was any conviction work-related?
+ Were any of the convictions for violent offenses against others?

What are your options? The most common and frequently utilized
option is to decline employment based on the fact that the candidate
lied on his or her job application. Most job applications will contain
a question that reads something like, "Have you ever been convicted
for anything other than a minor traffic violation?" Most people who
have a criminal record hope no one will do a check. The sad part
is, more often than not, no one will.

The way most candidates are eliminated, therefore, is not because
of the conviction, but because they lied about it on their job application. It's the lie, not the conviction, that usually eliminates the job
seeker from further consideration. As the person responsible for doing
the hiring, any sort of lie, either direct or by omission, should be
sufficient for you to move on to the next candidate.

Whether or not a candidate can be eliminated from further consideration solely on the basis of the conviction depends on the laws
of the state in which the employer is located. So, caution should be

used if that conviction is the primary basis for not hiring someone. In many states you can refuse to hire someone for that reason alone. But care still needs to be exercised, because in every state, under federal law, you have to be sure that a policy to deny employment does not have a "disparate impact" on a protected group, such as a racial minority. You should keep track of how many minorities are being denied employment because of a conviction, to ensure that your policy does not have a disparate impact on that particular minority group. That's why a statement like "A conviction will not necessarily bar you from employment. The type of conviction and when it occurred will also be considered" should follow the question cited earlier: "Have you ever been . . . ." The best advice is to check the laws in your particular state if you're going to deny someone a job solely because of a prior criminal conviction.

While there are pros and cons regarding the usefulness of a court check, it goes without saying that court checks should be done. We'll discuss these and other methods of obtaining information in the next chapter.

# ANCILLARY CHECKS: HOW TO SUPPLEMENT YOUR RESEARCH

As a subset to reference checking, there are a variety of ancillary checks available to anyone who wants to make sure the best hiring decisions are made. Think of these ancillary checks as confirmation of the accuracy of the basic information about the candidate. All of them normally have value when used in conjunction with reference checking. Their effectiveness, however, varies widely and is generally limited to the truthfulness or accuracy of whatever's being checked or verified.

Keep in mind as you read through this chapter that none of them, standing alone, address the central questions about job performance, either past, present, or future. Furthermore, none of them, standing alone, provide sufficient information upon which to base an employment decision. Instead, they work best when multiple checks are used, and, of course, when they are used to supplement the information you gather through the traditional reference check.

There are, broadly speaking, two ways of looking at the pre-employment checking exercise. Some employers simply want to get off as inexpensively as possible in order to show that "something"

was done prior to extending a job offer to avoid any future allega-
tions of negligent hiring. Others take the more expansive view—
that the more you know about a prospective employee, the better. If
you're responsible for hiring people, it just makes good sense that
the more you know about the people you're considering for employment, the better your hiring decision will be. Of equal importance,
you will have also clearly demonstrated that enough was done to
ensure that no one can accuse you of being negligent in your hiring
practices, regardless of who's doing the hiring and regardless of the
type of job to be filled. This more-is-better philosophy not only
applies to employers, but to anyone who is employing people for
just about any task or service to be performed. The negligent-hiring
question may not apply to a lot of service jobs that you have to fill,
such as an in-home health care provider or selecting a new minister,
but the philosophy of more is better is still the same. Why? Because
it just makes good sense. The same is true for landlords who are
evaluating prospective tenants. Collecting as much crucial information as possible may not be the easiest or quickest way to make a
hiring or leasing decision, but it's clearly the safest way to do it.

The way to make the most out of ancillary checks is to make sure
the ones you select are relevant to the position to be filled. In other
words, if the position to be filled really does require the candidate
to be a CPA, verifying that fact makes awfully good sense. Doing
a motor vehicle check is a very logical thing to do for employees
who will be driving a company-owned vehicle. In a similar manner,
if you're hiring a cashier, doing a credit check is clearly in order.
The point is, the choice of the ancillary checks you use needs to
relate to the requirements of the position to be filled. They can add
significant value to your knowledge base about the candidate and
help ensure that a good hiring decision is made.

Many employers will use a combination of ancillary checks, such as verifying academic credentials or a court check, as a prescreening technique to make sure that the candidate meets the basic job requirements before continuing with the interview or reference-checking part of the preemployment exercise. Evaluating the appropriateness of an ancillary check, therefore, can be extremely useful to tailor the preemployment screening package to fit the requirements of the job. This chapter provides an understanding of the various checks available to you and how to use them as you screen job applicants.

## COURT CHECKS

More and more employers want to do a *court check* to find out if a candidate for employment has a criminal record. Sounds like a sensible thing to do, considering the realities of the world in which we live, doesn't it? And it *is* sensible. Although the term *court check* is something of a misnomer, what we're really talking about is finding out if a candidate for employment or a prospective renter has been convicted of a crime. Depending on the nature of the conviction and the requirements of the job to be filled, a court check may be the determining factor in an employment decision. A court check can be a basic screening device to make sure that people seeking employment don't have a criminal record. But there are some fundamentals you need to understand first in order to make good use of a court check.

The first thing to understand is what it means to have a criminal record. Broadly defined, having a criminal record means you either pled guilty to or were found guilty of having committed a *crime*. Acts are crimes because they have been defined as such by the state, via some elected legislative body. Within that list of acts defined as crimes, some are viewed as being more serious than others. As a result, these acts have more severe penalties attached to them. They are commonly referred to as *felonies*. Less-serious crimes are called *misdemeanors*. The only difference between the two is the severity of the penalty for committing them. But, technically, being convicted of either a felony or misdemeanor means you have a *criminal record*.

Before going further, let's look at the most basic and fundamental facts about how to do court checks—what you're likely to find and not find and what bearing a previous conviction could have on an employment decision. First of all, *there is no single database where anyone can go and perform a nationwide court check.* The only nationwide database that exists is at the National Crime Information Center (NCIC), but for all intents and purposes, it can only be accessed by law enforcement agencies and a few business classifications such as airlines and banks, and then only on a need-to-know basis. Even at that, the NCIC database is only as good as the information supplied to it by the states and by local courts. So, if anyone tells you that he or she can do a nationwide court check for you, be advised, it just ain't so. OK, in theory it is possible to do a nationwide court check, but it can only be done one court system or one county at a time, and clearly this is a heroic and impractical task. Some states do have databases of convictions they collect from individual counties and judicial districts, but they are "passive" systems that depend on the willingness of court clerks to send in the information, because there are no current laws requiring that all conviction records be sent to a central collection agency. In many jurisdictions, the clerk of courts will only send in conviction records when asked to do so by a local law enforcement agency, so most state conviction databases are neither complete nor up-to-date.

So how do you go about doing a court check that reasonably addresses the question of whether or not a candidate for employment has ever been convicted of a crime? It's one thing to say you're going to do a court check; it's quite another to define what that will mean. As a practical matter, is it *ever* possible to say with absolute certainty that an individual has never been convicted of a crime? No. So what can you do? You can use reasonable care. That means doing a felony and misdemeanor court check in every county in which the person has lived within the last seven years. To be extra careful, include every county in which the person has worked during that same time period (assuming the counties of residence and employment are different). To go beyond that becomes impractical and cost-prohibitive. It makes no sense to check every court in every county in every state; and besides, realistically it can't be done. So should court checks be done at all, since they're not conclusive? Yes, absolutely. By checking counties of residence and employment, you'll have clearly shown that reasonable care was used to avoid hiring someone with a criminal record.

How do you perform a court check? Well, you could physically go to the courthouse and look, but there are several agencies that will, for a very reasonable fee, do court checks for you. If you want to do a court check yourself, all you have to do is go to the Clerk of Courts office in the local county courthouse and tell one of the deputy clerks that you would like to do a court check on so-and-so (some counties have all their records on computer, so it's a very simple exercise to type in the required information; others still use docket books where entries are made by hand). The Clerk's office is responsible for keeping the records of all felony and misdemeanor convictions on file.

If you want to use an outside agency to do the court checks for you, just go to your computer and use any of the search engines available. Then type in the words "court checks," and you'll find plenty of vendors happy to conduct the court check for you. Court checks ordinarily cost anywhere from $5 to about $20 per county and take a couple of days. There are some exceptions, however. Some states require payment in advance and the use of their form, which has to be sent by regular mail and can make a court check take as long as two or three weeks to receive. Keep in mind, however, that allowing the extra time is certainly worth the wait if by doing so, you discover that you're about to hire a convicted felon or someone with a history of workplace violence. The point is that it's better to wait a little while and be safe than to ignore the check and be *very* sorry later.

In summary, doing a series of targeted court checks is a relatively inexpensive way to make reasonably sure that a prospective employee doesn't have a history of criminal convictions and hasn't lied to you on his or her job application. Doing a court check, in other words, is simply a very prudent and worthwhile exercise.

## CREDIT CHECKS

Another tool that may be used in association with a full reference check is a credit check. In a nutshell, a *credit check* is a summary of money a person owes to others. Normally, lending institutions, credit card companies, and retailers who extend credit to their customers use credit checks. Lots of employers also use credit checks as a way to screen job seekers out of further consideration for employment. The notion is that credit-worthiness can be a predictor of how well that person will perform on the job. This concept, however, is debatable. Why? How can anyone possibly infer things like management style or ascertain skill sets or core competencies from a credit report? Well, you can't. There are only two reasons to ever do a credit check:

♦ If the nature of the position requires it. For instance, if you're going to hire someone who will have access to company funds, financial records, or the combination to the vault, it would be appropriate—and reasonable—to have a credit check done, because a candidate who's having serious financial difficulties could be tempted to access company funds for personal gain or to fend off creditors. Furthermore, if a candidate can't manage his or her own personal finances very well, it's not reasonable to assume that he or she would do any better handling company funds. For landlords, credit checks are an even more valuable tool to have because they will provide important information about how reliable a prospective tenant will be in terms of paying the rent consistently and in a timely manner.

♦ A credit check is appropriate if you have reason to believe a candidate's financial position might adversely affect his or her ability to do the job. For instance, if financial difficulties could result in court-ordered wage garnishments imposed on the employer, or if the candidate is going to be spending a significant amount of time away from the job dealing with collection agencies or being in court, that would be a reasonable thing to know before making a hiring decision. Otherwise, using a credit report to evaluate a candidate's eligibility for employment is a waste of time and money. The point of collecting credit information is for lending institutions or other businesses that extend credit to customers to evaluate whether or not the candidate's a good credit risk—that is, whether or not he or she is able to make the payments or repay the debt incurred.

Here are the things a credit check contains: It will disclose every place where a person has lived and also applied for credit, such as applying for a credit card, car loan, personal loan, or home loan. If a job seeker lived in a community and didn't apply for credit, that community won't show up on the credit check. It will contain a summary of how much money is owed on credit cards and bank loans. It will show credit limits, civil litigation involving credit, collections, and bankruptcies. It will also show past-due or late payments on credit cards or loans. It will show the type of loan, such as installment or revolving. It will show how much is owed, the terms of payment, and how much the payments are. A credit check will also disclose if any other credit checks have been requested on that particular person. Not all of this information will be relevant to the prospective employer. The purpose of this section is simply to tell you what credit reports contain.

For landlords, a credit check can be a *very* useful tool in evaluating prospective tenants. For example, if a prospective tenant has a history of being involved in a series of court-ordered garnishments or has taken bankruptcy, a landlord would be wise to think twice about renting to a person who has a history of not paying bills. A large debt load could also suggest that it will be very hard for the prospective tenant to make rent payments on time. The results of the credit check could very well be the deciding factor in whether or not you agree to rent property to someone. If, however, you make the decision to not rent an apartment or to require a higher deposit, for example, based on the information contained in a credit report, you'd be well advised to notify the prospective renter of the name and address of the agency who prepared the credit report and of their right to dispute the accuracy or completeness of any information furnished by the credit bureau, as well as their right to ask for a free copy of the credit report within 60 days.

In summary, should a credit check be run on every person seeking employment? No, only if the position to be filled requires it, or if there is reason to believe that money problems will have a negative effect on job performance. Credit checks can be done for a fee by any of numerous credit bureaus located in nearly every major city, which can be easily located by consulting your yellow pages or by using an online search engine. Ordinarily, a credit check can be done within 24 hours and will cost between $15 and $20.

## MOTOR VEHICLE CHECKS

Here's another auxiliary tool that may be useful. Actually, the term *motor vehicle check* is a little misleading. What we're really talking about is the status of somebody's driver's license, which can be determined through each state's Bureau of Motor Vehicles.

Driver's license checks are particularly important to do if you're planning to hire someone for a job that requires the use of a car as part of the job or if a new employee is going to be given a company car to drive. If, for example, you're planning to hire a chauffeur for your wealthy Great-Aunt Harriet, it might be nice to know that the best candidate has a valid chauffeur's license and doesn't have a string of previous convictions for speeding or driving while intoxicated!

The most common reason to do a driver's license check is for employers who are hiring people who will be driving for them as part of their job responsibilities. It's an inexpensive exercise, and when used in conjunction with careful reference checking, it can further reduce the specter of negligent hiring litigation for failing to check something so easy to verify. To carry out a check, you'll need the candidate's full name (as it appears on the license), date of birth, social security number, address, driver's license number, and state of issue. A motor vehicle check will ordinarily take two to three days, depending on the state.

Motor vehicle record searches need to be done in the state that issued the license. A signed release that complies with the requirements of the Fair Credit Reporting Act (if you don't have a release, your corporate attorney can easily prepare one, or if you're a small employer, any competent attorney could draft one for you) is necessary from the prospective employee, and in many states, the individual holding the license must complete a special form to obtain the record. (The easiest and least expensive way to do it is to require the prospective employee to get a copy of his or her own driving record.)

There is usually a fee to obtain the record, no matter who's getting it, and it varies from state to state. Ordinarily, if you use an outside agency to do the check, the fee to get a driving record can be from about $10 to $30. To initiate this process, all you need to do is contact your state Bureau of Motor Vehicles, which can easily be done by calling directory assistance and asking for the number, which is usually found under the heading of "state government," or by doing a search on your computer. Having the candidate provide a copy of his or her own driving record is one of the easiest approaches to take, however. The process is exactly the same, only easier. Have the candidate contact the state Bureau of Motor Vehicles and obtain a certified copy of his or her own driving record. No releases need to be signed and no permission granted, since the candidate is merely requesting a copy of his or her own driving record.

If you're the prospective employer, there are no special questions that need to be asked because a motor vehicle check will tell you the status of the person's license, if it's valid or not, if it's restricted for any reason (like poor eyesight), and if it's suspended for any reason. It will also show any traffic offenses the driver has committed, such as speeding, reckless driving, or driving while intoxicated. It will show past suspensions or restrictions, as well as the type of license, such as an ordinary driver's license, a commercial license, or chauffeur license.

## SOCIAL SECURITY TRACE

With identity theft becoming an increasingly serious problem, verifying someone's identity has become a very hot topic in nearly every hiring arena. A *social security trace* means verifying that the person claiming a number is really the person to whom it's been assigned. To do a social security trace, an employer must contact the Social Security Administration. Their number is in the telephone book under the general heading "US Government." Provide the employer's ID number, the name of the candidate, the social security number claimed, and the gender and date of birth for that person. If the information is correct, the Social Security Administration will confirm it; on the other hand, if something is amiss, they will request that the person being checked contact them. They will not tell you the number is invalid or to whom it really belongs. You'll know there's a problem if the Social Security Administration tells your candidate to contact them. Your role as the employer should be to withhold any offer of employment until the issue has been resolved. Depending on the nature of the problem, the delay could only be a few days, but if it's a serious problem, it could take months to resolve. There is no fee associated with a social security trace unless it's done through an outside agency. The typical fee is between $15 and $20. One of the nice things about doing a social security trace is that if there aren't any problems, the results are almost instantaneous.

An obvious problem for employers is avoiding an accusation of age discrimination because a date of birth is requested. The solution is to notify job seekers that the information is required for identification purposes only and will not be used, in any way, as a factor in determining eligibility for employment. With so much concern these days about identity theft, doing a social security trace is a very sensible, inexpensive, and reasonable thing to do. The risk, in other words, of hiring someone who is claiming to be someone else is far greater than the risk of being accused of age discrimination— especially if the employer states that requesting a date of birth is only for identification purposes.

Remember, the Social Security Administration will not provide any information about whose number is whose, nor would we want them to. All they will do is confirm that the information you provided is accurate. Ordinarily, a social security trace is completed when you make the call.

## VERIFICATION OF LICENSES

As a general rule, every license, no matter the type, should be verified. In my experience, doing license verifications is one of the easiest, but most often overlooked, types of checks available. More and more occupations require a license to offer particular services— everything from doctors and lawyers to CPAs, teachers, airline pilots, and scores of other occupations. The point is, whatever type of license a job seeker is claiming, it should be checked to ensure that it is currently valid without any restrictions or limitations on it.

Unfortunately, the more respected the occupation, the less likely employers are to check the validity of the license associated with it. This is particularly true of physicians. Because, as a society, we hold doctors in such high regard, many employers are reluctant to run the risk of insulting a physician by verifying a license to practice medicine. As noted earlier, the failure to do so can be potentially disastrous. All that's required is to place a call to the state agency that issues the license, whatever it's for, and to verify that it's valid. It's a quick, inexpensive, and very important step—regardless of whether you're the hiring manager of a Fortune 500 company or looking for a new family doctor. If a license cannot be confirmed for any reason, the most fair thing to do is inform the candidate and give him or her a chance to prove the license is valid. The proof, incidentally, should come in the form of a certified document from the issuing institution or agency. Again, any offer of employment should be withheld until the matter is cleared up to your satisfaction.

It's also important to keep in mind that there is some information that verifying a license *won't* tell you. I'm reminded of the old joke that asks, "What do you call the person who graduated dead last in his medical school class?" The answer: "Doctor." Verifying that an individual really is a physician says nothing about his or her skill, ability, or medical expertise. The same is true of every other occupation that requires a license. Being a licensed pilot doesn't necessarily mean that person is a *good* pilot. Do you see the difference? While it's important to verify that the individual does have the license claimed, doing so doesn't say anything about the overall ability to *do* the job. That's why checking references is still at the heart of the hiring process. There's seldom a charge to verify a license, and it can be done quickly with a simple telephone call.

## VERIFICATION OF ACADEMIC CREDENTIALS

While verifying the validity of licenses is the most overlooked step in the hiring process, falsifying academic credentials is the most common deception by far. Many otherwise qualified people think they need a little extra edge that claiming a degree will give them. They're willing to take a chance, in other words, that nobody will check to see if the degree claimed was ever actually conferred. Regrettably, in many instances, no one does check.

For the job seeker, claiming a degree that was never earned is a serious error in judgment, because it's so easy to verify. My experience has been that most employers are not nearly as concerned about the grade point average (GPA) of the individual as they are about whether or not he or she has that sheepskin. And besides, it isn't possible for an employer to obtain an official transcript of an individual's actual grades anyway. If you want to see a transcript of academic performance, the job seeker is the only person who can get an official copy of it from the college or university. But simply verifying that the degree was earned is a simple matter of calling the registrar's office and asking for confirmation. To do that, you only need a few things: the name under which the person attended school, the year the degree was allegedly awarded, and the type of degree claimed, such as B.S., B.A., M.S., or M.B.A..

For that handful of schools that won't confirm academic credentials, one of the tricks of the trade for reference checking is to call the school's alumni office and ask them to do it. As noted earlier in this book, part of the reason alumni offices exist is to help their graduates get jobs. I have never seen one unwilling to, at least, confirm that the job seeker is listed in their directory as having received the degree claimed. Another way to confirm academic credentials is to put the burden on the candidate to produce a dated copy of the official transcript or a copy of the diploma for you, which you then send back to the school for confirmation of its validity.

Speaking of tricks of the trade, it would be a disservice to the reader to not point out that a whole industry exists for the sole purpose of producing genuine-looking but phony diplomas. Seeing the diploma isn't enough. You need to actually call the school for confirmation or, as just noted, send the school a copy of the diploma for verification. There is also a book called *The Guide to Background Investigations,* published by National Employment Screening Services, that lists all accredited two- and four-year colleges and universities, along with current contact information. If a job seeker lists a college or university that isn't in *The Guide*, that should be the first red flag to go up. If it isn't listed in *The Guide*, it probably doesn't exist or it isn't an accredited school—still a red flag. *The Guide to Background Investigations* may be purchased from T.I.S.I., 4110 S. 100th East Avenue, Tulsa, Oklahoma, 74146. It's also available on disc. Both the hard copy and the disc are approximately $100, but it's well worth it if you're verifying a lot of academic credentials.

Now, let's look at what confirmation of academic credentials *won't* tell you. It will not tell how well the job seeker performed while in school. All confirmation of a degree will reveal is whether or not the person holds the degree claimed, not what sort of student he or she was. There is one exception to that, however. If a job seeker graduated with honors, that can be confirmed because that's how the degree was conferred. The usual academic distinctions are *cum laude*, *magna cum laude*, and *summa cum laude*. Roughly translated, they mean "with praise," "with great praise," and "with greatest praise." If a candidate claims to have graduated "with honors," that can be confirmed right along with confirmation of the degree itself, and it does mean that the job seeker did perform quite well academically.

Most of the time, there is no charge to verify academic credentials, either through the registrar's office or the alumni office. However, a few schools have outsourced the confirmation of academic credentials to an agency that charges a few dollars to confirm the degree claimed.

## PAPER-AND-PENCIL CHECKS

The term *paper and pencil* used in connection with any sort of aptitude or personality instrument is an antiquated description, but it's still a commonly used term. What we're talking about, no matter how it's administered, is a test that requires job seekers to answer a series of questions designed to measure a wide array of skills, inclinations, proclivities, and tendencies for nearly every field of human endeavor. There are tests for leadership, stress, personal style, written and verbal communication skills, verbal reasoning, numerical ability . . . well, you name the skill set and there's at least one test that will evaluate it.

As with all things, some evaluative instruments are better than others. The best have been validated over time and are excellent predictors of the things being tested. Paper-and-pencil tests are a great way to focus in on the strengths and weaknesses in areas of concern to the employer. For instance, if you're looking for someone with exceptional leadership skills, there are tests to evaluate how inclined that person is to be an effective leader, and more often than not, these tools will enable the prospective employer to tailor skill-specific questions that can be asked during that part of the preemployment process. Tests are also an excellent screening device to ensure that the basic qualities sought are already in place before moving forward with the hiring process. What they don't tell you is how those basic qualities will play out in association with others. For instance, if a leadership test indicates quite clearly that a job seeker has strong leadership skills, what it won't disclose is how that person will interact with other, equally strong leaders. Put in simplest terms, paper-and-pencil tests can tell you what the job seeker is like as an individual, from any of a number of points of view. But they don't necessarily reveal how that person has performed as part of a larger group over time.

For instance, if an individual is a strong leader, there's no way to know how that person has performed in the past in a subordinate role. Sometimes our natural proclivities, talents, inclinations, and aptitudes are controlled by external factors, not the least of which could be previous work environments, the particular responsibilities of a job, or the personalities of others with whom we have been required to work. Depending on the type of test being administered, the cost to the employer can range anywhere from as little as $10 to as much as $500 per candidate. There are dozens of firms offering testing services, and they can easily be found on the Internet. Results can be obtained instantaneously, if it's done online. Normally, test results are available within a week to 10 days.

Paper-and-pencil tests, therefore, are excellent tools to use, but to maximize their benefit, they need to be used as a guide for directing the content of the conversations held with people with whom the job seeker has actually worked. For instance, suppose an evaluative instrument indicates that the candidate is very strong-willed. Armed with that knowledge, you could ask a reference, "How would you describe so-and-so's flexibility in terms of his/her willingness to change his/her mind?" By doing that, it's possible to really get a more complete view of an individual—not just at one moment in time, but over the course of a period of time and from different points of view.

In this chapter we have taken a close look at the major ancillary checks available to employers. They all have value in the hiring process, but their real value comes when they are used in combination with an objective assessment of past job performance, and that can only be done by checking references. Some ancillary checks should be done on every job seeker. They include, at least, court checks and the verification of licenses and academic credentials. Then, depending on the requirements of the position to be filled, other checks can be added to address the special circumstances associated with the particular job.

# CHAPTER 8

# COMMON REFERENCE-CHECKING MISCONCEPTIONS

If you'll recall, in the introduction to this book, I suggested that one of the problems in the reference-checking field is the lack of any fundamental understanding of the meaning of the terms we use to describe the preemployment process. It should come as no surprise, therefore, that the process of checking references is clouded even further by misconceptions, folklore, and legends about what you can and can't do. The purpose of this chapter, therefore, is to explore—and explode—some of the myths that surround reference checking and to tell you, the person doing reference checks, the way it *really* is.

## "EMPLOYERS AREN'T ALLOWED TO DISCLOSE ANYTHING EXCEPT JOB TITLES AND DATES OF EMPLOYMENT"

Frequently, hiring professionals encounter HR people who make statements like this: "Employers aren't allowed to disclose anything except job titles and dates of employment."

Regardless of which side of the employment fence you happen to be on, a pervasive notion exists that says employers, somehow or other, aren't *allowed* to disclose much of anything about former employees. Well, at face value, that statement is false. Of course, employers are allowed to disclose more than that. They may elect *not* to disclose more information by adopting a policy that forbids disclosing anything more than job titles and employment dates. But there's no hard-and-fast rule, external to the company, that applies to every employer, under all circumstances, and at all times. Ultimately, most would agree that, policy notwithstanding, employees are disclosing more anyway. In other words, they ignore the policy.

For those companies who do have a no-comment policy, it's clear their legal departments have advised them to adopt it. Why? Because of the perceived fear that if employees are free to say anything else, the company will be putting itself at risk of being sued for defamation. The assumption is that employees are more likely than not to intentionally, or unintentionally, lie about their former colleagues, which is absurd—particularly if the job seeker has asked a colleague to serve as a reference and the colleague has agreed to be one. So, some employers take the stance that simply confirming somebody actually worked for them is about all they feel safe in saying. Actually, I have encountered employers who decline to do even that much! I have talked to HR people unwilling to confirm that the candidate being checked ever worked there at all. It's one thing to be cautious, it's quite another for a company to be afraid of it's own shadow. I recall a conversation that went something like this:

"Hi, I'm calling to confirm that so-and-so worked for you as a design engineer from April 1996 to September of 2001."

The answer came, "I'm sorry, we're not allowed to disclose that information."

"But so-and-so said he worked there during that time, and I'd just like to make sure the information is correct."

"I'm sorry, we are not allowed to disclose any information of that type."

"OK, here's the situation. So-and-so is the primary candidate for a senior design engineer's position with a company we represent. If I can't confirm that he worked for you, it's likely that he won't be hired. I don't want to know why he left or how he did while he was there. I just want to know if he worked there when he said he did. Can't you at least tell me that?"

"No, that's our policy, and I can't violate it."

"Do you realize how much this is going to hurt so-and-so's chances of getting this job?"

"I'm sorry, I can't help that." Click.

As far-fetched as this example may sound, it's pretty close to a word-for-word transcript of what actually happened. What can you do if you run into someone like this who follows company policy to the letter? The easy solution is to go right back to the candidate and ask him or her to give you the name of someone else willing to simply confirm the dates of employment and job title. Admittedly, this is an unusual situation, but it *can* happen.

Now, my question is, what possible harm could have resulted from merely confirming that person's job title and dates of employment? Unless the person with whom I was speaking had intentionally lied about the job seeker, the answer is, absolutely nothing. Assuming the candidate being checked told the truth about where he worked, how long he was there, and what his job title was, where's the potential harm to the former employer in saying so? In my view, it's a gross disservice to those good former employees who are working hard to find other employment.

No matter what anybody tells you, there are no laws proscribing what an employer can say about former employees. The distinction that confuses people is between a *policy* adopted by the employer and a *law* passed by a legislative body. Policies are the rules a company adopts that outline things such as how many vacation days employees are allotted or how many paid sick days employees may take. When a legislative body meets and decides to control how fast you can drive your car, and attaches a fine or other penalty for driving in excess of that speed, that's a law.

So, in a nutshell, employers are allowed to disclose whatever they choose to disclose. And, as long as whatever is said is an honestly held opinion or a documented fact, there is no liability for saying it. You may be reprimanded for saying it if there's a *policy* that forbids it, but you certainly won't go to jail.

Now that we've made that distinction, let's move on to what you, as a prospective employer, can do to get around the policy-followers within an organization. We've already established that the more information you can collect about a candidate for employment, the better. Now, what can you do to confirm employment and also assess the candidate's overall job performance, along with the candidate's suitability for the job you want to fill?

The key is to remember that the employee selection process has a certain interactive quality about it. It's not just a matter of taking a résumé or job application and doing all the work yourself while the job seeker sits patiently by the phone waiting to be offered a job. People seeking employment have a responsibility to facilitate the process of being hired, too. As we have noted earlier, the responsibility for accessing the information you want (and *need* in order to make an informed employment decision) rests squarely on the shoulders of the job seeker.

There is another way to get around employers' misguided beliefs that they should only reveal job titles and dates of employment. You can bypass the HR department altogether. Even if the company has a stringently enforced policy about only disclosing the bare minimum, put the burden on the candidate to find people who *will* talk. One of the best ways to do that is to suggest that the candidate recruit people who've retired from that company or taken other jobs to serve as references. They will be able to, at the very least, confirm employment. And in all likelihood, they will be great references.

But let's go beyond the myth that there are universal rules that apply to all employers. What about the myths surrounding job performance?

## "IT'S 'ILLEGAL' TO PROVIDE JOB PERFORMANCE INFORMATION"

Once again, this is a popularly held belief among many employers that just isn't true. There are no laws that have criminalized providing job performance information about current or former employees. As we've discussed, there are *civil* consequences if a reference intentionally lies about a job seeker, but it's certainly not a crime and it's certainly not illegal. This myth has come about because employers misunderstand the terms being used. We'll get into a thorough discussion of the legal issues and how they apply to the hiring process in significantly more detail in Chapter 10.

If an employer intentionally lies about a former employee by saying a good employee performed badly or by saying a bad employee performed well, that employer could be sued. The job seeker could sue the former employer in the first instance, or the hiring company could sue the former employer in the second. Keep in mind, however, particularly if you're the one doing the hiring, who's likely to be sued by whom.

If every reference says, in one form or another, that the candidate isn't right for the job (and as a result you decline to make that person a job offer), are you the one likely to be sued? No. If anybody's going to be sued, it will be one or more of the references the candidate supplied to you in the first place. And how likely is that? I wouldn't have much confidence in a candidate's judgment if he or she asked people to serve as references whom he or she didn't believe, in advance, would offer a fair assessment.

Actually, I'd be more inclined to expect his or her references to overstate skills and abilities, rather than understate them. That's really where the art of reference checking comes in—getting past the "halo effect" from references who think they're helping the candidate get the job by offering excessively glowing comments. The way to get past the halo effect is to probe beyond the glittering generalities by asking for specifics. For instance, if a reference says the candidate was the best employee her company ever employed, ask for examples. One way to do it is to say something like, "That's great to hear. Could you give me some examples of how so-and-so's performance was so exceptional?" Ask for specifics that will back up the generality. Remember, nobody's perfect, and we can all improve in some way, so a "glittering generality" has to be challenged, but in a positive and nonjudgmental way.

More importantly, the burden of proof would be on the candidate to show his or her own references intentionally lied about him or her. Once again, however, the point is there are no laws that make it "illegal" to discuss past job performance.

Let's look at a theoretical example. Suppose you're an employer and you want to hire a new process engineer, or a personal accountant, or even a babysitter, for that matter. Also suppose that you've narrowed the field to the top three applicants, based on their résumés, interviews, and any other preemployment tool you care to include.

Let's call the candidates Tom, Dick, and Mary. Then suppose you ask each one for a list of at least three references. You specify that you require all of the references to be people for whom they've actually worked with in the last five to seven years. Moving on, let's suppose you carefully check all the references provided and conclude that among the three finalists that Tom's overall job performance has been good, but not great; that Dick's performance has been consistently substandard; and that Mary is by far the most experienced and best performer among the group. So, naturally, you offer the job to Mary and she accepts. What about Tom and Dick? As a practical matter, all you have to say to them, assuming you choose to say anything at all, is merely that you've filled the position. You don't have to tell them why or go into any detail at all about the basis for your decision. At most, you could say you found someone you felt was more qualified for the job. Have you told them the truth? Yes, you have. Are they entitled to any more information about how you reached your decision? No, they're not. Ninety-nine percent of the time this theoretical example is exactly how it will go.

For the sake of discussion, though, let's say Dick decides to sue one or all of his references for, he supposes, saying bad things about him that caused him to lose the job. His references will show up in court and produce performance evaluations that clearly document his job performance as being consistently substandard. And the next thing you'll hear is, "Judgment for the defendant. Case dismissed."

For some readers, the prospect of facing litigation may sound like it adds credibility to enforcing a strict no-comment policy. Aside from the injustice this does to good employees who want to advance their careers on the one hand, and employers who get stuck with poor performers who just happen to interview well on the other hand, the fact of the matter is that, strict no-comment policy notwithstanding, employers are doing it anyway!

## Another Problem Associated with Encountering a "Company Policy"

There is another side to the company policy ploy that employers shouldn't overlook. Over the years I have found that people listed as references will occasionally cite a real or imaginary company policy to avoid saying anything negative about a former employee. The interesting twist is that the very thing they want to avoid saying is often true. You just have to get at it. The easiest way to do that is to go right back to the candidate and explain what happened and ask the candidate to ask his or her references to respond to the questions asked, or to supply alternate references who will respond to the questions asked. Unless the candidate convinces his or her references to be more forthcoming or if alternate references aren't provided, the red flag that should have initially come up when the reference ducked behind "no comment" just got a lot bigger.

The point here is that a no-comment policy, while ostensibly intended to protect the company, can be a way for a reference to avoid revealing negative performance issues he or she knows to be true. "I liked Charlie. He was a good guy, but I really can't say much more than that because of company policy." Should that be a red flag if Charlie asked that person to be a reference for him? Yes, absolutely. How do you deal with that sort of comment if you're the prospective employer? Well, for one thing, this is why you check more than one reference. If the candidate provided the references himself and all three of them hide behind company policy, I'd not only be concerned about Charlie's judgment, but also, and more importantly, about Charlie's suitability for the position. If this sort of thing happens to you, and it will occasionally, I'd look for another candidate.

## "IT'S OK TO ASK REFERENCES ABOUT PERSONAL MATTERS—AS LONG AS THEY RELATE TO THE JOB"

No, it isn't. Personal matters are just that—personal. If you're planning to hire a female, can you ask her if she's planning to have children someday? No. Can you ask her about her marital status or her plans to get married? No. Can you ask any candidate about his or her overall health? No. All three of those questions fall under headings that are encompassed by the provisions of the Civil Rights Act of 1964, as amended.

"But," you say, "I don't want to hire someone who's going to miss work because of a preexisting illness or a female who is going to miss a lot of work while on maternity leave!"

At some level, those might seem like reasonable questions to ask, but if you *do* ask questions about health or marital status, you're directly violating federal law and you're just asking for a federal discrimination lawsuit to be filed against you. How people live their lives and what they do on their own time is none of your business—unless how they live or what they do on their personal time will adversely affect their ability to do the job. The example I like to give is, "It's none of my business if a candidate lives in a tree on weekends, unless that means he's going to fall asleep at his desk on Mondays!"

The way to deal with this issue is to simply ask, "Are you aware of any personal problems that could affect so-and-so's ability to do the job for which he's being considered?" If the answer is yes, just ask the reference to explain. Then, depending upon the answer—and the answers other references give to the same question—you'll have to decide if the problem, whatever it happens to be, is significant enough to disqualify the candidate from further consideration for the job to be filled.

## "BASING AN EMPLOYMENT DECISION ON A CREDIT CHECK IS ALL YOU REALLY NEED"

There is a school of thought subscribing to the notion that cheaper and quicker is always better. The problem, of course, is the inherent truth in the opposite notion that you get what you pay for—that is, spend as little as possible and you're likely to get as little as possible. Regardless of whether it's a credit check or a court check, neither is sufficient (standing alone or in tandem) to make an employment decision. I'm reminded of an employer I knew who was short of stature. If anyone significantly taller than this man applied for a job, he wouldn't hire him or her. Was that a discriminatory hiring practice? Well, in theory, you could make an argument for that, but legally speaking, tall people do not fall into a protected category. So this guy could, with impunity, decline to hire people strictly on the basis of height.

The point, here, is making a hiring decision based on nothing more than height is not all that different from making a hiring decision based only on a credit report or a court check. Neither approach makes much sense. The principle of more information is better than less information clearly applies. No matter how urgent the need, no matter how attractive the candidate may seem on paper or how skilled at being interviewed, there is no substitute for careful reference checking. Incidentally, my height-challenged friend certainly was spending less than even the "credit checks are good enough" crowd; you don't have to outsource height measurement to anybody! What it really amounts to is being penny-wise and pound-foolish. We know, for instance, that the cost of making a bad hiring decision—which is possible when only looking at a credit rating or somebody's *height*—is approximately three times the annual salary of the position. Does it make any sense to base a hiring decision on less rather than more information? No!

## "ONE REFERENCE IS GOOD ENOUGH"

Remember the more-information-is-always-better-than-less theme we've been developing? Checking one reference is never good enough. The idea behind careful reference checking is to look for *consistency* among the comments made by multiple references. It's pretty tough to find consistency in the comments of only one reference, not to mention the increased possibility that the comments from only one reference will be slanted in one direction or the other. The validity of reference checking can only come from talking to three references. That's how you compare and contrast comments and explore inconsistencies . . . and that's how you make a more informed hiring decision.

## "IF AN EMPLOYEE WAS REFERRED BY ANOTHER EMPLOYEE, HE MUST BE OKAY"

It's perfectly natural to assume that when one of your employees recommends someone for employment, he or she will do a good job, and to be candid, most of the time it's true. But there are those occasions where an employee is just trying to do a favor for a buddy who really needs a job, without thinking about the consequences. Common sense would seem to suggest that no employee would intentionally put his or her own job at risk by recommending someone who is more likely to fail than to succeed.

Another element that plays into this sort of situation is the possibility of a mismatch. The employee, trying to merely help a friend, recommends him or her for a position for which the friend simply isn't qualified . . . not a happy situation for any of the parties concerned. What to do? Well, first of all, any employer would be foolish not to be grateful for an in-house recommendation from an employee. The key, however, is proceeding with a careful reference check— just as though the prospective employee happened to walk into the personnel office by chance. Most of the time, recommendations like these work out, but like any hiring decision, it's far better to check and be safe than not to check and be sorry.

## "THE CANDIDATE GREW HER LAST COMPANY TO GREAT SUCCESS, SO SHE MUST BE GREAT!"

Remember the point about reference checking that one of the essential ideas is to evaluate past job performance over time? Or put another way, one success "doth not a career make." Of course, it seems logical to assume that if the candidate enjoyed great success in the past, she'll continue to be successful. But be careful. This misconception is an excellent example of precisely why careful reference checking is so important. There are just too many unknowns. What was the condition of the company before she took over? What style did she use? Would that same style fit the requirements of the job to be filled? What was the previous corporate culture like? Does it match the corporate culture of the prospective employer? Are the problems the same? Is growing the organization for the prospective employer the primary goal? If not, do they have another mission in mind? Will she be able to handle it with equal success? Well, I think you see the point.

There's no question about the fact that the candidate in this example comes to the employee selection process with a major success to her credit, but that's really all it says. The prospective employer needs to know a lot more about her before making the determination that she's the right candidate for the job.

## "THIS PERSON WAS FIRED FROM HIS LAST JOB, SO HE PROBABLY WILL BE A POOR CHOICE"

This is precisely the exact opposite of the previous misconception. Again, you can't blithely assume from a single piece of information that a prospective candidate, strictly on the basis of one termination, will be, by default, a poor prospect for employment. You need to know more. You need to know what caused the termination. Was it the job seeker's entire fault or was there more to it? Could there have been a new boss with whom this person simply couldn't get along? There could be a dozen contributing—and mitigating— factors that need to be taken into account. And the only way to do that is, again, by talking to multiple references. It's as natural, on the one hand, to assume that a termination means the candidate will be a poor employee as it is to assume, on the other hand, that a major success guarantees a great employee. Before any valid conclusions can be reached, more information is needed from people who were in a position to know the facts—and who are willing to discuss them.

One dramatic piece of job performance information, while important, is seldom enough, standing alone, to make the most informed or best hiring decision.

In this chapter we've looked at a few of the common misconceptions associated with reference checking and the preemployment process generally. There is a guiding principle, however, that everyone who hires people should follow: Use your common sense. If what you want to know isn't about past job performance, don't ask it. If you're using an outside vendor to do the checking for you, make sure you know the value of what you're getting. Some employers try to minimize the hiring costs and, as a result, have high turnover. Some spend more than they need to. My message in this chapter is that more information is better than less. Combine that with some of the tools we've already discussed, and you can improve your hiring practices dramatically. The bottom line, however, is always find out about job performance, job performance, and job performance.

CHAPTER 9

# THE CANDIDATE'S ROLE IN REFERENCE CHECKING

For any employer who is responsible for making hiring decisions, this chapter heading should pique your interest: "Do candidates have a role to play?" They most certainly do. In fact, if they *don't* have a major role to play, I certainly don't know who *would*!

For more years than I can recall, employers I've worked with have assumed that they're stuck with the references provided by a candidate for employment. To the extent that an employer is only permitted to contact references supplied by the job seeker—without running the risk of an accusation of invasion of privacy—employers *are* stuck with the references provided by the candidate. But only in a very narrow context.

Employers should not randomly contact anybody they can find on their own who has some passing acquaintance with the candidate and discuss with impunity past job performance—or any other aspect of the candidate's personal or professional life. If you, as the employer, happen to know someone who has worked with the candidate, you certainly could ask the candidate to include that person as a reference. By the same token, employers have *every right* to specify the *types* of references with whom they want to talk.

Job seekers, therefore, hold far fewer cards in this part of the hiring process than employers may think. If you're the employer, you have something the job seeker wants—a job. And for every candidate who, at first blush, might look like a good prospect, there are probably dozens of others standing in the same line waiting for the chance to work for you. So, first of all, let's dispel the myth that employers are stuck with contacting only those references who are provided by the candidate. The key is to insist that the candidate provide the types of people with whom *you* want to speak, *people with whom the job seeker has actually worked on a day-to-day basis within the last five to seven years.* Once you have that list, you're stuck with it, but that shouldn't matter if they're the right *types* of references.

## A MIX OF REFERENCES

We've already talked about the ideal set of references—a current or former superior, peer, and subordinate. We also acknowledged that supplying that mix of references isn't always possible. Nevertheless, every employer has the right, and the responsibility, to insist that people seeking employment provide *work-related references*, no matter what the nature of the association is—or was. For job seekers just beginning their careers, a major professor, advisor, or activity sponsor could all be appropriate references. For job seekers who have not gone to college, a counselor, teacher, or coach could fill the bill.

The idea behind asking for the mix of references is to be able to view the candidate from more than one perspective and over a period of time that's long enough to be illuminating. How a supervisor viewed the candidate's overall job performance last year may be entirely different from how a subordinate saw it last month. And both of those perspectives may be different from that of a former coworker who had a completely independent view of the candidate (because there was no direct reporting relationship).

It's also perfectly understandable that not every job seeker has had supervisory responsibility and, therefore, no one reporting to him or her. In that case, peers and supervisors will have to suffice, but the point remains the same: The prospective employer should be defining the types of references to be provided. If a candidate can't or won't come up with the names of people who fit that description, that should be a red flag of major proportions, and the employer should keep on looking for candidates who can.

## THE ARTFUL DODGE

Sometimes a person who has performed poorly, for whatever reason, will have what, on paper, appears to be a sparkling list of references who either don't know the candidate or if they do, know him or her only slightly, if at all. (What the job seeker is doing is betting that the prospective employer won't bother to check those references—and in truth, many times that's true. As a result, sometimes faking it can be a successful ploy for a job seeker with a less-than-desirable work history.)

The other extreme to which many marginal performers will go is to ask friends and relatives to pose as job-related references who, if called, will only offer glowing comments about the candidate. (It is precisely for these reasons that references should be checked and insightful questions asked to make sure the person at the other end of the line really is a valid reference—see Chapter 5 for techniques for determining someone's honesty.)

By contrast, job seekers who have performed well should be happy to provide the prospective employer with as many work-related references as requested. If the job seeker has done a good job and the people with whom he or she has worked know it, why wouldn't he or she want them to be references? The question, in many instances, is how to get them to do it. We've discussed the ruse about "company policy" and the unwillingness of potential references to cross that imaginary line long enough. If you're the prospective employer, it's the *candidate's* job to come up with work-related references who *will* talk to you. That's just a fact of life for a job seeker.

## ADVICE YOU CAN GIVE

Moving on, let's continue this chapter by discussing how you, as the prospective employer, can advise the job seeker on how to come up with work-related references who will talk to you—what they should say and what they should not say.

Here's the basic premise: Most of the time, people we work with for any length of time (usually a minimum of six months) become our friends. They move beyond the more formal category of "boss," "coworker," or "people who work for me," to the second, more personal category in human relationships called "friend." I can only think of one instance over the last 20-plus years when I've heard a job seeker claim that he had never had any friends at work. His contention was that he came to work, did his job, didn't socialize with anyone, and at the end of the day, went home. So much for his talent and expertise at interpersonal skills!

Once that transition from "coworker" to "friend" takes place, those folks become eligible to qualify for that third category, "reference." It doesn't matter whether the prospective employee currently works with this person or not, as long as the period of their association stays within the past five-to-seven-year time frame. References can include friends with whom the prospective employee worked who are now retired, who have taken other jobs, or who may have moved to other locations or business units within the same corporate organization. Actually, people who have moved on are really the best ones for job seekers to recruit as potential references. Why? Because they won't be constrained by that company policy thing we talked about in the previous chapter. They should feel perfectly free to accede to a request and serve as a reference.

## AVOIDING A MISMATCH

Remember, the object of the reference-checking exercise is to make sure that the candidate is right for the job and that the job is right for the candidate. If the job really isn't right for the candidate, for whatever reason, it's far better for you, as the prospective employer, to hear it from references than to hire someone for a job at which he or she will eventually fail. Failing is a lose-lose situation for both you and the job seeker. There is no positive outcome with a job mismatch. Additionally, being spared a job mismatch keeps the candidate's career on track and moving forward, which benefits both parties.

Two obvious, but often overlooked, things you should advise prospective employees to do once they've selected their references are as follows:

+ Have the candidate tell his or her references that they have his or her absolute *permission* to talk with prospective employers who call.

+ Tell the candidate to ask his or her references if they will talk to a prospective employer *directly* if called. If for any reason a reference starts to hedge or flat out refuses to talk to prospective employers, advise the candidate to pick references who will. Although it's hard to imagine that a friend and coworker would agree to serve as a reference, and then refuse to talk to a legitimate employer, it can happen nevertheless. And if it does, it's usually because the job seeker didn't make absolutely sure the reference would talk to prospective employers in the first place.

## THE TRUST FACTOR

There's another element of the reference selection process that job seekers shouldn't ignore, and that's the trust factor. If you're advising someone who's looking for a job who needs to line up references, tell the job seeker to make sure the references are *trustworthy* and, hopefully, loyal friends as well as coworkers of some sort. Friends, by definition, are supposed to be trustworthy, but that isn't always so. "Friends" developed in a social environment are sometimes of a different stripe than those acquired in the workplace. Considerable thought and good judgment is required in the selection of references. While you don't want references to overstate skills and abilities, you don't want them to understate a prospective employee's abilities either. Exaggeration in either direction is a disservice to both the job seeker and the prospective employer. Worst of all, it can lead to a job mismatch.

Now, what about the job seeker who has only worked at one place for an extended period of time? What if you, as the prospective employer, want to talk to at least one reference from the job seeker's current place of employment? If the prospective employee has essentially worked at only one place for the last 10 or more years and he or she doesn't necessarily want the employer to know he or she is looking for other opportunities, part of the same strategy noted earlier still applies. That is, tell the prospective candidate to identify people who've retired, taken other jobs, or moved to other functional areas within the company—people who can be trusted to keep not only the job search confidential, but who will also agree to serve as references.

If the candidate's best references are still with the current employer, however, then *trust* becomes the central issue. It's up to the job seeker to come up with references willing to talk from among those with whom he or she currently works. That means the job seeker will have to ask the appropriate people—confidentially—to be references. Here's a suggestion you can offer: The easiest way to enlist references is away from the workplace, over lunch, or after work some evening. If they are loyal friends—and only the prospective candidate can be the judge of that—they won't violate that request for confidentiality. By the same token, if those who are willing to be references are likely to feel uncomfortable discussing job performance while they're at work, advise the job seeker to see if they would mind receiving a call at home. Frequently, current references will be glad to talk to a prospective employer during the evening or on a weekend. Also remember to mention, again, that the job seeker is *not* asking references to speak on behalf of the company they both work for, but only to offer honestly held opinions about job performance—nothing more.

Now, what about the prospective employer who insists on talking to a current supervisor? What can the job seeker do if he or she doesn't want a supervisor to know he or she is looking? First of all, there is an unwritten rule that no prospective employer should ever jeopardize someone's current job. Most job applications, in fact, have a section that asks if the current employer may be contacted. If the prospective candidate doesn't want that to happen, he or she should just say "no," and that request should be honored without question. As an alternative, most job seekers ordinarily will have at least one friend/coworker who can be trusted—that's generally all that's needed. The other option for the job seeker is to provide plenty of other work-related references from among previously held jobs or that specialized class of individuals who have (1) retired, (2) taken other jobs, or (3) moved to other functional areas or locations within the company. You can also advise a job seeker to ask the prospective employer to delay calling the current supervisor until a job offer has been made. Some employers make job offers contingent on reference checking anyway. (Nevertheless, think twice about doing it this way, because if the offer is withdrawn, the candidate will know exactly what caused that to happen. Clearly, it will have been something said by one of his or her references.)

## CONTINGENT OFFERS

If the offer is made contingent on a background check, as we've come to know and define it in this book, then it's possible that a skeleton in the closet (the job seeker was hoping nobody would find) could be unearthed. But it's also possible that the job seeker has been mistaken for someone else. Mistakes do happen. For instance, there are a lot of John and Jane Smiths out there; credit bureaus, for example, sometimes report back on the wrong one. Another common mistake is to confuse a father and son who have the same name. Spelling errors can be made. Occasionally, credit information isn't up-to-date, and the problem that existed two years ago has been satisfactorily resolved. Lots of things could happen that may produce a questionable credit report. That's why the Fair Credit Reporting Act gives job seekers the right not only to be told that a background check is going to be done, but it also allows job seekers to see the results. (It could be that the person with the horrible credit history just happens to have the same name as the candidate.) Keep in mind, though, that the burden is on the job seeker to prove that he or she is not the person cited in the report.

There's another issue that needs to be addressed within the context of contingent offers based on contacting references: If the prospective employee is the one seeking out the references and providing them to the prospective employer, he or she ought to have a pretty good idea of what those references are likely to say. If he or she doesn't know, then the job seeker hasn't done a very good job of choosing the right references. But that's not to suggest that totally positive and honest comments by references will guarantee a job offer, either. For one thing, there are too many other factors employers consider. But if the offer really *is* contingent on what references say and the candidate doesn't get the job, it doesn't always mean one of the references sabotaged his or her job prospects. It could mean the candidate just isn't the right person for the job. Maybe you, as the prospective employer, are looking for a hands-on manager, and the candidate's references know he or she is much better at delegating authority to others. All it really means is that a probable mismatch has been avoided.

Before we close this chapter, let's review the steps that your potential employees should be taking in selecting references. This list should be useful to those who are not only seeking employment, but also as a guide for employers that can be offered to prospective employees. When it is time in the hiring process to ask for references, consider telling your candidates to adhere to the following advice. You may even want to give them a printout of the following list, which spells out the points that relate to their specific situations:

♦ Compile a prospective list of people you've actually worked with on a daily basis within the last five to seven years—8 to 10 names would be sufficient. (All you really need are three or four people willing to be references for you, but if more are agreeable, a longer list is perfectly acceptable.)

• Try to make sure that your list contains variety, in terms of the nature of your associations with prospective references. Your list should include, if possible, at least one superior, a peer, and a subordinate. Their associations with you should also cover a span of time so that the prospective employer isn't just calling people from your most recent job.

• Be selective in terms of whom you place on your list. Base the selection on such things as how well you know them, whether or not they're friends as well as coworkers, and how trustworthy they are. The more cordial the relationship, in other words, the better.

• Rank your list of prospective references based on how familiar they really are with the job you held, its responsibilities, and whether or not they would be likely to have an opinion about your performance. (It's nice to have the senior vice president on your list of references, but if he or she only saw you once a month, how much will that person really know about your day-to-day job performance?)

• As you're deciding whom your best references would be, also try to put yourself in the prospective employer's shoes and consider whom you would want to talk to if you were responsible for filling the position. Ask yourself what you'd want to know about *you*.

• Starting at the top of your list, call each reference, and specifically and directly ask the person for permission to use him or her as a reference. Explain why you're asking, and answer any questions the potential reference may have.

• If a prospect agrees, make doubly sure he or she understands exactly what you're asking them to do: that you don't want the prospect to overstate or understate how well you did your job, but to just answer every question as honestly as possible.

* If a prospective reference hedges or declines, accept it gracefully. (You really don't want someone serving as a reference for you who has any qualms about it.)

* Make sure your references know where you're applying, if possible, so they'll be able to make sure that calls are truly from the prospective employer or its agents *and*, most importantly, so they'll be *expecting* the calls.

* If you want your references to keep the fact that you're considering other employment opportunities confidential, ask them directly not to speak to anyone else about it.

* Advise your references that they should limit their responses strictly to job-performance-related questions. Any question that goes beyond that should not be answered. If the question isn't about job performance, it shouldn't be asked, and if it is asked, it definitely should not be answered.

* *Above all, make sure you provide all the current contact information for each reference to make sure it is reasonably easy for a prospective employer to reach them.* The information should include full name, current job title, company name and address, current office and home telephone number, and how you are/were acquainted with each one—for example, "Former superior at XYZ company from 1995 to 1999." Be sure to include the information where it is best to contact the reference at home or on the weekend. The easier you can make it for a prospective employer to reach your references, the better.

# CHAPTER 10

# LEGAL ISSUES TO CONSIDER AS YOU ARE DOING REFERENCE CHECKS

Before we even start this chapter, let's try to get past a little of the mystery that surrounds the law and the legal profession. As we've already learned, a company policy is not a law. Without trying to give legal advice, in this chapter, I'll outline a few more basic concepts that the non-lawyer responsible for hiring people must understand. Why? Because we need to demystify the law just a little so that you, as the person responsible for hiring others, have at least a rudimentary understanding of the legal issues that can swirl around the process. While some of the examples in this chapter may seem unrelated to hiring, they nevertheless illustrate an important legal concept that you should understand. So, let's start at the very beginning: For purposes of this book, there are really only two types of legal actions that people who hire other people need to understand: crimes and civil wrongs.

## CRIMES

An act committed by a person is a crime because we, as a society, have decided to define that act as a crime through our various state legislatures and through the Congress of the United States. You may recall the speeding example: Zipping through town at 90 miles an hour is only a crime because we've decided to define it as a crime—because it poses an unacceptable risk to public safety, obviously. Anybody can appreciate why that's so. To reduce that risk, we, the people, through our elected state legislatures have, by law, set speed *limits,* the violation of which has been defined as a crime. People who are alleged to have committed a crime find themselves in court, where the state is the complaining party (the plaintiff) and the person accused of committing the crime is the defendant. Within the framework of reference checking, it's very unlikely that you will ever be confronted with an allegation that a "crime" has been committed, but you still need to understand the broad meaning of the term, if for no other reason than to not worry about it.

## CIVIL WRONGS

The only other type of action we need be concerned with is lawsuits. Loosely defined (for simplicity's sake), a *lawsuit* is a civil action where the contending parties are two individuals. For example, I believe that I didn't get the job because I think you were playing favorites and hired your nephew instead of me. I then sue you because I think I was wronged. I become the complaining party (the plaintiff), and you become the defendant. Companies and corporations can also be parties in civil lawsuits. The complaint in this example isn't a *crime*; it's a *civil wrong.* The way you avoid becoming a party to a civil action is to use "reasonable care" in the hiring process. What constitutes reasonable care will be explained later in this chapter.

One of the most common misconceptions is that somehow the mere act of *asking* a question that could be discriminatory is illegal. Well, it's not illegal to ask anything of prospective employees. For instance, if you ask a job seeker's age and you base part of your hiring decision on the answer, you could become a party to a civil action alleging age discrimination, but it's not illegal to ask. It's not even illegal to act on the information, but it's very likely that you could be sued. However, you still haven't broken any laws. That's why it's fundamentally important to understand the difference between a crime, which it is illegal to commit, and a civil wrong, which involves two parties, one of whom has been wronged. In this example, the employee who was not hired because of age has been wronged and can file a civil suit for damages.

## LAWSUITS GENERALLY

As I have noted, there are few words in the English language that strike terror in the hearts of HR people more than the word *lawsuit*. Let's try to de-terrorize it. A lawsuit, for our purposes, is essentially a civil complaint by a person or corporation that claims it has been wronged by some other person or corporation. There is no question about the fact that, as a society, we've become lawsuit-happy. The legal profession must accept part of the blame for the proliferation of frivolous lawsuits, but part of the blame, also, must be placed on insurance companies. And there's no doubt that many lawsuits are filed by individuals who just are not willing to accept that they might be to blame for what happened to them.

Personal-injury litigation, for example, is one of the most common types of lawsuits, because most people have insurance to protect themselves from liability for injuries to others that could be considered "their fault." Here's a simple example: You invite a job candidate to your office for an interview. After the interview, the candidate trips and falls down the stairs. He sues your company for the medical expenses incurred, because, so the theory goes, the company was at fault (negligent) for not making sure that the stairs were safe and caused him to fall. Your company has a liability insurance policy that covers this sort of thing. The insurance company, rather than go to court and fight over the amount of the claim for medical expenses or whether the candidate should have been more careful, will often agree to pay a settlement out of court because settling the claim is cheaper. Lawyers know that. So, the candidate's lawyer collects as much as half of the amount the insurance company agrees to pay the candidate for the medical expenses, and the candidate gets the remainder.

The truth of the matter is anybody can sue anybody else, but that doesn't mean the complaining party is always going to win. A word also needs to be said about what the lawyers in the corporate legal department are being paid to do. Whenever a question with potential legal consequences is sent their way, their mission—and to some extent, their responsibility—is to look at the worst thing that could happen and try to reduce that risk to the greatest extent possible. Lawyers, in other words, are really the risk managers for a lot of companies. Here's how all this plays out in the HR departments of many American companies: When the discussion turns to reference and background checking, the legal department creates a comprehensive "no comment" policy for the HR people to hide behind to avoid the perceived risk of lawsuits. The less you say, in other words, the lower the risk of being sued—or so the thinking goes.

Obviously, if we're in the business of hiring people, regardless of the venue, some risk is going to be involved. Let's look at the major legal issues and see if they can be put in some commonsense perspective.

## NEGLIGENT HIRING

Generally speaking, *negligent hiring* is the failure of an employer to use reasonable care in the selection of an employee that results in injury to an innocent third party. We've talked about this before, but because this "civil wrong" exists, you need to be fully aware of it. The way to minimize the risk of being accused of negligent hiring is to use reasonable care in the hiring process. The key, therefore, is to have a general understanding of what "reasonable care" means. Volumes have been written about the evolution of the meaning of the phrase, but from the standpoint of employers, it should be enough to say that collecting more information about a candidate for employment is always better than collecting less.

Let's also look at this from another perspective. Many times, employers have been found liable for the actions of their employees because they "knew or should have known" about an employee's history of, let's say, violent behavior in the workplace. A very simple illustration may make these words of legal art easier to understand.

Suppose you're responsible for hiring a doctor for a medical clinic. Let's say you've identified a candidate who you've interviewed and upon whom you've had a court check and a credit check done. Let's suppose you've even talked to a couple of references. Now suppose you hire the doctor, and in the course of performing his duties, he injures a patient and your clinic is sued. Your defense will be based, at least in part, on the steps you took during the preemployment phase of the process. But for the sake of this example, let's say that the doctor had lost his license to practice medicine in your state. It is very likely that the injured patient will prevail because you "knew or should have known" that the doctor's license was suspended. In practical terms, you should have called the state board of medical examiners to verify that the physician had a valid license. In other words, you could have found that out by making a simple call. By not checking the license, did you fail to use reasonable care in the hiring of that doctor? In all likelihood, the answer would be yes.

What constitutes reasonable care will vary, depending on the potential risk of harm to innocent third parties. The standard of reasonable care, in other words, will be much higher for our ubiquitous brain surgeon than it will be for a custodian. Determining what a reasonable standard of care will be for every job classification may seem like a daunting task, and it could be, unless you remember that collecting more information rather than less is always better—even for the custodian.

It should also be kept in mind that the word *harm* isn't limited to the everyday notion of physical harm. Harm to an innocent third party can be economic harm, psychological harm, or a dozen other types of harm. The point, ultimately, is that it's never appropriate not to check anything on a candidate for employment. Checking nothing would constitute negligent hiring on its face.

## NEGLIGENT REFERRAL

*Negligent referral* is a relatively new civil wrong that may contradict the policies that many HR people have always believed. In the proverbial nutshell, it is the failure of a former employer to disclose information about a former employee that leads to the injury of an innocent third party. Negligent referral represents a whole new line of cases that, in effect, say former employers have a duty to at least be honest in their comments about a former employee—so much for the safety of hiding behind a no-comment policy. The only way—at the moment—to avoid the specter of negligent referral litigation is not to reveal anything!

Let's walk through another theoretical example. Suppose you're the employer and you fire someone for workplace violence. You receive a call from a prospective employer asking why that individual left, and you say, "Oh, he resigned," or you say, "I suppose he thought he could get a better job elsewhere," *knowing* that he was fired for violence in the workplace. Suppose that individual is hired and injures a coworker at his new place of employment. Now let's say the new employer sues you, claiming that you failed to disclose the real reason for that individual's departure and alleging negligent referral. There is now precedent that would lead a jury to conclude that you were negligent because you, in effect, knowingly lied about the reason for the departure. Guess who's going to pay? You are! This example brings us back to a point we've visited before: Honesty is *always* the best policy. If you fire a candidate for a valid reason, it's perfectly fine to disclose that reason if you're asked—because it's *true*. And even if you should happen to be sued by the employee who was fired, claiming he was denied employment because of what you said, you will prevail because "the truth is an absolute defense."

## BURDEN OF PROOF

As previously noted, one of the goals of this chapter is to provide some understanding of the legal concepts involved in the hiring process.

Whenever we talk about lawsuits, the term "burden of proof" inevitably comes up. What, in everyday terms, does that phrase mean? Let's suppose you're the employer and a prospective employer has called you about a former employee. You disclose that the former employee was caught stealing from your company and was fired as a result—which is true—and because of that, the former employee doesn't get the job and decides to sue you. The burden of proof is on that former employee to prove that you maliciously and intentionally lied about her, not the other way around. In other words, she has to prove you lied; you don't have to prove you told the truth. And just what level of proof must that former employee reach to make her case against you, as the former employer? I hate to do this, but there are a couple of legal phrases that are useful to understand. In a *criminal* case, the burden of proof is on the state to prove that the defendant committed the crime "beyond a reasonable doubt." Over the centuries, that phrase has come to mean that if even the slightest doubt remains as to whether or not the defendant committed the crime, the verdict must be "not guilty."

In a *civil* action, the plaintiff—in our example the person who didn't get the job—must prove that you intentionally and maliciously lied about her "by a preponderance of the evidence." The level of proof in a civil action is much lower, in other words, than in a criminal action. "A preponderance of the evidence" means the plaintiff must show to a degree of something like 51 percent certainty, or that it was "more likely than not" that you intentionally and maliciously lied about her and, as a result, she was wrongfully denied employment. Keeping in mind that the burden of proof is on her, she'll fail because she really was caught stealing and was fired.

## LEGAL PROTECTION FOR EMPLOYERS

At this writing, over 40 states have passed legislation limiting the liability of employers who disclose information about former employees that results in former employees being denied employment, *as long as the information is true*. The protection a majority of the states has provided does not, in other words, extend to employers who maliciously and intentionally lie about former employees. In spite of that, many employers still feel the necessity to institute no-comment policies with regard to responding to inquiries from prospective employers about former employees. So, clearly some new layer is needed for employers to feel safe allowing the disclosure of more than the old "name, rank, and serial number."

Michael Blickman, one of the leading employment attorneys in the country, with the highly regarded Ice Miller law firm in Indianapolis, has written, exclusively for this book, a brand-new, groundbreaking release. Every employer should have every current employee who is departing the company sign this document. The document releases the employer from potential liability for allowing current employees to serve as references. The idea is essentially the same as the release prospective employees sign *prior* to employment that allows the employer to contact references before a job offer is made. The only difference is this new release is signed *before* the departure of the individual from the company that allows a future employer to call references still with the company. All the employer has to do is insist that employees who have been asked to serve as references by the departing employee provide either honestly held opinions or state documented facts that relate exclusively to past job performance. This new release should eliminate the need to ever have a no-comment policy again!

139

## STATEMENT OF POLICY ON REFERENCE REQUESTS AND EMPLOYEE'S AUTHORIZATION AND GENERAL RELEASE AGREEMENT

*What is the Company's general policy on reference requests?* In the event the Company receives a request for information or a reference about a current or former employee (hereinafter collectively referred to as "Employee"), our general policy is to provide only neutral information, such as the Employee's employment dates and his/her position. Exceptions to this general policy may be made by the Company at its sole discretion.

*Will the Company provide more than neutral information about an Employee if he/she authorizes it?* Yes. We realize that an Employee may want us to provide more than neutral information about him/her to a prospective employer. Providing such information can be very helpful to an Employee's prospective employer. This additional information can assist that employer in making a decision as to whether to offer employment to that individual.

Businesses adhere to neutral reference policies because of the concern over possible defamation lawsuits or other legal actions that may result if an Employee fails to obtain a job because of what his/her former employer said to the Employee's prospective employer. Whether or not this concern is well founded, companies that provide information to others about Employees undertake a risk that can be avoided by simply saying nothing or just providing neutral information.

While the vast majority of companies adhere to a neutral reference policy, we want to provide each Employee with an opportunity to authorize us to provide information, in the addition to the above, about him/her to a prospective employer. We believe that companies should be encouraged to share information about their employees with prospective employers. However, in view of the current risk in doing so, we will only provide additional information about Employees (beyond the neutral information discussed above) on the basis of the understandings and agreements described in this document, which includes a broad and binding waiver and release of all claims against the Company and any prospective employer receiving information from it.

*What will the Company advise its employees in regard to reference requests about me?* We will advise our employees who are asked to serve as references to provide only honestly held opinions and/or documented facts. They will be further advised to only respond to questions that relate specifically to the Employee's employment history with the Company, including his/her past job performance.

*Is an Employee required to sign this document?* No. It is up to each Employee to decide whether or not he/she wishes to sign this document. No Employee is required to do so. Each Employee's decision must be voluntary and with an understanding of the effect of signing the document. Each Employee should address any questions to the Company's Director of Human Resources.

\* \* \*

**EMPLOYEE'S AUTHORIZATION TO COMPANY TO PROVIDE INFORMATION AND GENERAL RELEASE AGREEMENT**

READ CAREFULLY: THIS IS A RELEASE OF ALL CLAIMS

I, the undersigned, hereby voluntarily sign this Employee's Authorization to Company to Provide Information and General Release Agreement ("Release"). In signing this Release, I authorize the Company to provide any and all information about me to any prospective employer or other individual or entity seeking a reference about me. Such information may be provided by it in writing or orally. I understand that the information that the Company may disclose includes, but is not limited to, a description of the various positions I held with the Company; my various duties and responsibilities; the circumstances relating to my separation and/or resignation; and information about my performance and/or accomplishments while employed by the Company. I understand that the Company will exercise its sole discretion regarding the nature and extent of the information it will provide about me. I understand that I cannot make any representation to any prospective employer about the nature or extent of information that the Company may provide to it about me because this is the Company's decision.

I also understand that the Company has made no promise to me that the information it will provide about me will be positive, negative, favorable, unfavorable, helpful, or unhelpful. No agent of the Company is authorized to make any such promise to me, and none has done so. The Company has the right to provide information about me that it deems appropriate, in its sole discretion, as stated above. Therefore, I understand that the information that may be provided by the Company about me may assist a prospective employer in determining whether to offer employment to me. However, I also understand that such information may result in a prospective employer's decision not to offer employment to me. I understand that the Company cannot make any guarantee or promise to me regarding the result of providing information about me to a prospective employer. I have not asked the Company to guarantee or prom-ise any such result, nor have I received any guarantee or promise from the Company regarding the information to be shared about me or regarding the result of sharing such information. Moreover, I have no right to obtain from the Company any description or details about the information it shares about me. I fully recognize that if I fail to obtain any future employment or incur any injury or damages as a result of any information provided by the Company, I will have no right to make a claim or file a lawsuit against the Company, its agents, or its representatives, even if they or any of them caused me not to gain employment or to incur injury or damages.

In consideration of the Company's willingness to consider providing information about me to a prospective employer, which I acknowledge is adequate and valuable consideration to support this Release, I hereby irrevocably and unconditionally release the Company, its current or former affiliates, and their employees or agents, and any person or entity to whom information about me is disclosed by the Company (collectively, the "Released Parties") from all known or unknown claims that I may have now or in the future relating to or arising out of the disclosure or use of any information that the Company provides about me to any prospective employer or to any other person or entity seeking a reference about me ("Claims"). The Claims I am releasing include, without limitation, claims under Title VII of the Civil Rights Act of 1964; Section 1981 of the Civil Rights Act of 1866; the Americans with Disabilities Act; any tort, including, but not limited to, defamation, slander, and libel; breach of contract; any blacklisting or similar law; any law that may provide me with a cause of action against the Company as a result of sharing information about me; and any other federal, state, or local common law, statute, regulation, or law of any other type. I acknowledge that I am releasing Claims I know about as well as Claims I may not know about. I understand the significance of releasing Claims I may have. I agree that I will never file any lawsuit, complaint, or charge against the Released Parties based on the Claims released in this Release. In the event I institute any legal or other action against any of the Released Parties with respect to any Claim waived by this Release, the responding party will be entitled to recover from me all damages, costs, expenses, and attorneys' fees incurred as a result of that breach. I agree to pay the reasonable attorneys' fees, costs, and any damages any of the Released Parties may incur as a result of my breaching a promise I made in this Release (such as by suing any of the Released Parties over a released Claim) or if any representation I made in this Release is false.

By signing this release and waiver of claims, I am releasing and waiving any claims against not only the Released Parties, but also any prospective employer that I have and any entity or individual seeking a reference about me, and their agents, in connection with the receipt and use of the information provided by the Company. As stated above, I expressly acknowledge that the information that may be provided about me by the Company may be positive, negative, or neutral in nature, and that neither the Company nor any agent of the Company has made any promise, guarantee, or representation to me in that regard.

I acknowledge that, before signing this Release, I was given at least seven calendar days to consider it. I further acknowledge that: (a) I took advantage of that time to consider this Release before signing it; (b) I carefully read this Release; (c) I fully understand what this Release means; and (d) I am entering into it voluntarily. I further acknowledge that the Company encouraged me to discuss this Release with my attorney or other advisor (at my own expense) before signing this Release and that I did so to the extent I deemed appropriate.

This Release sets forth the entire agreement between me and the Company pertaining to the subject matter of this Release. This Release may not be modified or canceled in any manner except by a writing signed by both me and an authorized Company official. I acknowledge that the Company has made no promises to me other than those in this Release. If any provision in this Release is found to be unenforceable, all other provisions will remain fully enforceable. It is not necessary that the Company sign this Release for it to become binding upon both me and the Company. This Release binds my heirs, administrators, representatives, executors, successors, and assigns, and will inure to the benefit of each of the Released Parties and their heirs, administrators, representatives, executors, successors, and assigns. This Release shall be construed as a whole according to its fair meaning. It shall not be construed strictly for or against me or the Released Parties. Unless the context indicates otherwise, the term "or" shall be deemed to include the term "and" and the singular or plural number shall be deemed to include the other. This Release shall be governed by the common law and statutes of the State of _____ , excluding any choice of laws statutes or common law.

[For California employees, add the following:]

This Agreement shall be effective as a full and final compromise and settlement of any and all of My Claims. In furtherance of this intention, I hereby waive any and all rights and benefits which I may have under Section 1542 of the Civil Code of the State of California, which provides as follows:

*Certain claims not affected by general release.* A general release does not extend to claims which the creditor does not know or suspect to exist in his favor at the time of executing the release, which if known by him must have materially affected his settlement with the debtor.

I hereby expressly waive and relinquish any rights or benefits which I had, now have, or may have in the future under Section 1542 of the Civil Code of the State of California, or any similar provision of statutory or nonstatutory law, to the fullest extent that I may lawfully waive any such right and benefit pertaining to the subject matter of this Agreement. In this regard, I acknowledge that I am aware that I or my attorneys may hereafter discover claims or facts in addition to or different from those which I now know or believe to exist with respect to the subject matter of this Agreement, and it is my intention to fully, finally, and forever settle and release all possible claims I may have against Company for or relating to the subject matter of this Agreement. Further, it is expressly understood that notwithstanding the discovery or existence of any such additional or different claims or facts, the releases given herein by me shall be and remain in effect as a full and complete release with respect to all claims released hereunder.

\* \* \*

   TAKE THIS DOCUMENT HOME, READ IT, AND CAREFULLY CONSIDER ALL OF ITS PROVISIONS BEFORE SIGNING IT. THIS DOCUMENT INCLUDES A RELEASE OF KNOWN AND UNKNOWN CLAIMS. IF YOU WISH, YOU SHOULD TAKE ADVANTAGE OF THE CONSIDERATION PERIOD AFFORDED BY THIS RELEASE AND CONSULT YOUR ATTORNEY.

Have you read and do you understand everything in this document?

If so, initial here: ____

Do you understand you may consult an attorney or other advisor before signing it?

If so, initial here: ____

Have you signed this document voluntarily?

If so, initial here: _____

Printed Name_____

Signature_____ Date_____

Received by the Company on the following date: _____

By: _____

Title: _____

[**Author's Note to Readers:** The Release does not include a release of claims under the federal Age Discrimination in Employment Act, which covers employers with 20 or more employees. That law prohibits the release of claims that arise after the effective date of the release document signed by the employee. ]

### Disclaimer

The preceding document is designed to provide information and guidance in regard to the subject matter covered in this book. No representation or warranty is made regarding the effect or enforceability of the document in any legal action. In publishing this book, and including the above material, neither the author, the publisher, Ice Miller, nor Michael A. Blickman, Esq., is engaged in rendering legal or other professional service. If legal advice or other expert assistance is required or desired, the services of a competent professional should be sought. In addition, before using the preceding document, readers should seek legal counsel to discuss the effect of any applicable federal, state, or local laws or regulations on the document.

Now, for the first time, legal protection is available on both sides of the hiring equation—for the former employer and prospective employer. By having the departing employee sign the new release, former employers are released from liability for what their employees say—as long as they offer honestly held opinions or state documented facts. (And if you're the candidate, why would you ever ask anyone to be a reference for you who you thought would intentionally lie about you in the first place?) For prospective employers, all you have to do is have candidates for employment sign the standard release (found in Chapter 4) that gives you express permission to contact the candidate's references and anyone else who would be familiar with his or her past job performance. For everyone concerned—the former employer, the job seeker, and the prospective employer—with two documents, we have made it possible to offer legal protection to everyone involved in the reference-checking process.

Of almost equal significance, you should note that we have finally come full circle in at least one sense. Earlier, the point was made that former and prospective employers should be free to exchange information about people seeking employment, just on the basis of common sense and common business practice. Now we have wrapped that common sense in the mantle of legal protection that should facilitate the process of making universally better employment decisions.

Before we leave this subject, however, you may be wondering why anyone would bother coming up with a new release that makes it possible for employers to allow their employees to serve as references at all. Because, if the truth be known, *employees are serving as references for people with whom they've worked anyway*. Employers might as well face the fact that their employees are serving as references in spite of company policies that forbid it. That's just a fact of life. If that's the case, and we know it is, why not add that extra layer of legal protection? Let employees serve as references, as long as the departing employee signs the new release. While no written release can ever be bulletproof, using this release allows employers to release themselves from 99 percent of the fear of liability they have lived with for so long.

Finally, what if the departing employee won't sign the release, for whatever reason? The solution is simple; the employer should stick with the no-comment policy.

## WHICH IS THE GREATER RISK? BEING SUED FOR FAILING TO CHECK OR BEING SUED IF YOU DO?

At this point the answer to the preceding question should be clear: Employers are at far greater risk of being sued for *not* checking than they are if they carefully check both backgrounds and references. Not checking is very much like hiring people directly off the street and taking them at their word that they have the experience, training, education, and skills to do whatever the job happens to be, and hoping that they've told the truth.

The only basis for being sued if you check references and backgrounds of candidates for employment is invasion of privacy. However, so long as you've made sure that your candidates sign a comprehensive waiver giving you express permission to check, the chances of being sued drop nearly to zero. Of course, it's still possible to be sued for basing an employment decision based on a response to a discriminatory question (refer back to the section of Chapter 4 for what *not* to ask).

On the other hand, negligent hiring litigation is becoming more and more common. Failing to use reasonable care in the employee selection process leaves the lawsuit door wide open for nearly any type of harm an unchecked employee may cause to others—especially when it can be shown that the employer could have reduced the risk of harm by carefully checking. It's really not possible to have too much information about a prospective employee, and, of equal importance, job seekers who are who they claim to be and can do what they claim they can should be universally happy to check whatever you, the prospective employer, feel is appropriate so they can get that job offer. All this amounts to is just common sense placed within a legal context.

## THE FAIR CREDIT REPORTING ACT

The Fair Credit Reporting Act was created to prevent the abuse of consumer credit information in connection with extending credit to people by institutions like banks, credit card companies, retailers, and other institutions offering credit to consumers. Over the years the Federal Trade Commission (FTC) has interpreted, reinterpreted, and redefined the provisions in more ways than are worth going into here.

The point is, if you're an employer and you use a consumer reporting agency to provide an investigative consumer report on a candidate for employment, and you base your hiring decision "in whole or in part" on the information contained in that investigative consumer report, there are certain things you *must* do:

◆ First, you have to tell the job seeker that you're going to have an investigative consumer report done by a consumer reporting agency (generally, we're talking about a credit report here).

◆ If you do use a consumer reporting agency, you must obtain the prospective employee's signature on a form that discloses legally required information to him or her.

◆ Before you decide not to hire the job seeker based in whole or in part on the results of any of those checks, you have to notify the job seeker, in writing, of the name of the consumer reporting agency and provide copies of any of the materials you received from the consumer reporting agency. This gives the unsuccessful job seeker a reasonable opportunity to refute or correct any of that information which may be false or incorrect.

◆ Then, after you decide not to hire the job seeker, the law requires that you advise the person in writing of that decision and give him or her yet more information about the consumer reporting agency and the individual's rights. For instance, suppose you have a credit check done on a candidate for employment as a cashier (a logical thing to do), and based on that check, you decide *not* to hire that person (let's suppose the candidate's name is Jane Smith). The reasoning behind the disclosure requirement is to give Jane the chance to show that the credit bureau got the wrong Jane Smith, which is possible, and sometimes really does happen. Again, the burden is on the candidate to show that the Jane Smith checked is really another person who just happens to have the same name—that's the point of the exercise—to help prevent people from wrongfully being denied employment on the basis of incorrect, out-of-date, or inaccurate information.

Keep in mind that the provisions of the Fair Credit Report Act only apply in those situations where you, as the prospective employer, have hired a consumer reporting agency, like a credit bureau, to do a credit check for you. If you're just doing your own reference and background checking—not a credit check—you do not have to disclose the results of the reference checks.

Here's a simple illustration of what usually happens: You, as the employer, tell a candidate that you check references and backgrounds. In the course of doing the background check, you discover that the candidate falsified his or her academic credentials—no question about it. You tell the candidate that you were unable to confirm the degree. Nine times out of ten, that's the last you'll hear from the candidate, because the candidate knows he or she has been caught. Of that remaining 1-in-10 candidates who insist that the degree is valid, it's up to him or her to prove it, through a certified transcript or some other means that you can verify. Mistakes do happen, but not all that often. And, if you decide not to accept the explanation he or she gives you, that is totally up to you.

Taking a more expansive view, the FTC has extended the consumer credit protection notion to include people seeking employment—not just people applying for consumer credit, such as a bank loan. To the extent that it's appropriate, there's no reason not to disclose the fact that background information is going to be checked. As far as references are concerned, the job seeker should know whom you're going to contact. Having talked to those references and concluded, let's say, that the candidate's management style doesn't fit the requirements of the position you want to fill or that the candidate's interpersonal skills aren't very good, you *do not* have to disclose that to the candidate.

In summary, in this chapter we've talked about a variety of legal issues that surround the hiring process. I've tried to explain, in everyday English, some of the terms uncommon to non-lawyers and how they affect the employment process. Mostly, this chapter has been devoted to putting the legal issues within a practical context that anyone can understand and, hopefully, to take some of the inherent fear out of the word *lawsuit*.

# CHAPTER 11

# HOW TO BE A REFERENCE

At first glance, the subject of this chapter might seem, well, shallow. How hard can it possibly be to serve as a reference for someone? All you have to do is answer a few questions and you're done, right? Not necessarily. Are there questions you *shouldn't* answer? How candid should you be? What about the consequences of violating company policy? Are you allowed to offer your opinion? How do you know the call is really from an employer interested in hiring the person for whom you've agreed to be a reference? All of these factors, when taken together, make knowing how to be a reference for someone a little more challenging.

## HOW TO MAKE SURE THE CALL IS LEGITIMATE

Let's switch sides of the fence for the purposes of this chapter and discuss what happens when you, the reader, serve as a reference for someone with whom you've worked. Now let's suppose you receive a telephone call from someone purporting to be a prospective employer. How can you know it's a legitimate call? Believe it or not, there are companies out there that job seekers can hire to find out what sorts of things their references will say about them. What these companies do is try to give the impression they're an interested employer when, in fact, they're working for the job seeker to "preview" what you'll say about them before they list you as a reference. It's also not uncommon for job seekers to ask a friend to call and pretend to be an employer for the same purpose—to find out what sorts of comments you'll make. So, how can you tell if the call is on the up-and-up?

Generally speaking, however, what usually happens is a friend with whom you've worked will ask you to be a reference and tell you that someone will be calling. Ninety-nine percent of the time the call will be from the actual employer, but if you're not sure, the following steps are simple safeguards you may want to utilize.

There are some very simple ways to make sure you are talking to a legitimate employer. The first question you should ask yourself is, "Has so-and-so asked me to be one of his or her references?" If the answer is yes, then at least you know why you're being called, but you still don't really know if the person calling is a legitimate employer or not. If you were asked to be a reference, but you still doubt the authenticity of the call, you can ask the caller for his or her name. Also ask for the name of the company he or she represents, for the company's location, *and* for a phone number where he or she can be reached. Then, depending on your own comfort level requirements, say you'll have to call him or her back in a little while. All you have to do is call Directory Assistance for the main number of the company, call it, and ask for the person who called by name.

If you're immediately connected, you'll know the initial call was real and you can proceed with the interview. If it's an agency, ostensibly working for the prospective employer, ask for the same information and follow the same steps, except when you call the main number, ask what their company does. If they're a search firm, employment agency, or even a company that does the reference checking on behalf of employers, then you can proceed to ask for the person who initially called and proceed with the interview. The third thing you can do when you receive a call about which you're not sure is simply call the person who asked you to be a reference in the first place and have him or her confirm the identity of the caller by asking for the name of the company and where it's located. Then you can call Directory Assistance and get the company's main number. Call it to double-check not only what the company does, but whether or not the caller is really employed there.

One last safety measure you can take is to ask the person calling to fax you a copy of the waiver signed by the candidate granting the prospective employer—if that's who's calling—permission to contact references, provided that company has implemented a waiver policy in its hiring process. Once you have that waiver, it won't matter whether or not the call is legitimate. All you have to remember is to only respond to questions about past job performance and to make sure you're only providing honestly held opinions or documented facts. In other words, just be honest. Once you have a copy of that waiver signed by the candidate, you can safely call back knowing that even if the caller isn't legitimate, you're still covered.

## WHAT ABOUT COMPANY POLICY?

Now let's suppose that you and another person have worked together for the last, say, five years. And let's also say that the two of you are good friends, not just at work, but socially too. One day this person comes to you and says something like, "I just had a great call from the XYZ Company, and they're considering me for a job that would mean more money and a promotion. They check references, and I'd like your permission to mention your name." You know that there's a strict company policy barring employees from giving out any information about current or former employees. What do you do? Do you refuse to serve as a reference for your friend and maybe cost him/her the chance of advancing his/her career? Do you violate company policy and run the risk of being fired if you're caught? Do you duck the call? Do you refer the whole matter to HR?

We already know that many people who are asked to serve as references ignore company policy. They feel justified in going ahead and accepting a legitimate reference call. But if you find yourself in the quandary I've just described, here's what you can do: Ask the prospective employer to call you at home, and make it crystal clear that you are *not* speaking on behalf of the company, only on your own behalf. So in a sense, even though you're clearly serving as a business or professional reference, being called at home tends to make the call take on a more personal character that should put you at ease both in terms of helping a friend and not overtly violating company policy. After all, calls you receive at home aren't anybody else's business.

## WHAT QUESTIONS ARE LEGITIMATE?

For what appears to be a simple question, the answer is somewhat complicated. Technically, you should only respond to questions about job performance. Some employers are interested in more than that, but your responses should stay focused on job performance. There are two ways to handle questions that go beyond job performance:

♦ Don't answer it, and make a point of saying that you feel the question is inappropriate because it's not about job performance.

♦ Respond to the question within the boundaries of job performance, even if it's asked more broadly.

For instance, suppose you've agreed to serve as a reference and you get a legitimate call from a prospective employer—just the way it's supposed to work—and you're asked the question, "How would you describe so-and-so's interpersonal skills?" Your response should be to clarify, "You mean on the job?" Or, you can qualify your response and say, "His/her interpersonal skills *on the job* were . . . ."

It goes without saying that questions about the candidate's personal life are off-limits. The only way you should ever respond to questions about someone's personal life is if some aspect of it impacts his or her job performance. If you've been asked to be a reference, and you've agreed, and a prospective employer calls and asks you something like, "Does so-and-so have a drinking problem?" here's what I would strongly recommend. Assuming that so-and-so *doesn't* have a drinking problem that affects his or her performance, say, "I'm not aware of any outside issues that have had any impact on so-and-so's job performance."

Most people who call you as a reference will know what they should and shouldn't ask, but some clearly will not. From your standpoint as a prospective reference, the simplest thing to remember is this: If the question has nothing to do with job performance, don't answer it.

## THE TRUTH IS AN ABSOLUTE DEFENSE

I recently gave a speech to a group of HR people. During the course of the presentation, the following comment was made: "When I have to fire someone and that person asks me what I'm going to say if a prospective employer calls, what should I do?"

My answer was, "Tell the terminated employee that you're going to tell the truth."

The questioner replied, "I've done that, and people just go ballistic when I tell them I'm going to be honest."

If that were the only question asked by a prospective employer, I could understand (and sympathize with) the employee's concern. But the point is, responsible reference checking involves asking a lot more than why someone left a job. And in many instances, a termination is not necessarily reflective of job performance *over time*. My experience has been that careful reference checking will usually reveal patterns of on-the-job behavior. To put it another way, one termination doth not a career ruin. The important thing to remember when serving as a reference is to tell the whole story and to tell it honestly.

People are terminated every day, but that doesn't necessarily mean they'll never be hired again. The important thing to know is what caused the termination. Here's an example: One of our clients wanted to hire an inside salesperson. All the references were essentially positive, but there was some question about this individual's ability to do cold selling. The client was aware of that possibility, but he felt his company's training program could teach anybody to become a productive salesperson. Well, in this instance, the sales training just didn't take. The individual who was hired simply wasn't comfortable doing cold selling to total strangers. No matter how hard he tried, he just couldn't do it. As a result, he was terminated. Was that termination tantamount to an employment death sentence? Not at all. The individual had performed extremely well in many other aspects of the job and was well liked by everyone. This was just one of those instances, as we've discussed, where it was simply a job mismatch.

Furthermore, two of the man's coworkers even agreed to be references for the guy. In less than a month, he was hired for a job that turned out to be a good match, with no cold selling.

If you think about this situation from the standpoint of the references, all of them essentially provided honest opinions about the candidate. The first employer knew about the possibility of failure doing cold calls; they simply guessed incorrectly about the impact of their training program on the candidate's job performance in that one area. The second employer talked to at least one reference who knew about the termination, but he had the expertise to ask what caused it. Even though it was a termination, the result was a far better job match on the second try. Honesty clearly paid off for the candidate in the long run. So, even a seemingly negative, but honest, comment has to be viewed within the context of everything that is said by each reference.

Sometimes people who are asked to be references feel an obligation to give the person who's looking for employment a glowing recommendation. Honesty, however, is always the best approach. It's just as harmful to the job seeker to intentionally overstate past job performance as it is to intentionally understate it. Overstatement or understatement—both are a gross disservice to the candidate *and* the prospective employer. From a legal standpoint, intentional overstatement or understatement could also lead to a lawsuit based on negligent referral or defamation.

That's why the title of this section, "The Truth Is an Absolute Defense," is so important if you're going to be a reference for someone. Suppose you know an employee was fired for, let's say, stealing. Are you putting yourself at legal risk by disclosing that fact to a prospective employer? No! Just as long as the statement is true you have what lawyers call "an absolute defense." Carrying this example a little further, suppose you disclose the termination for stealing, and as a result, a prospective employer denies the job seeker employment. Then suppose you get an irate call from that job seeker who says, "You kept me from getting that job because you told them I was caught stealing, I'm going to sue you!" (Remember, it is the threat of being sued that causes many people to be unwilling to serve as references in the first place.)

Here's what's likely to happen: Let's assume the disgruntled job seeker goes to see his lawyer and explains what happened. Any reputable attorney is going to ask, "Well, is it true that you were fired for stealing?"

"Well, yeah, but my reference told the prospective employer and I didn't get hired. I want to sue him!"

"Well, you can sue, but you'll lose because your reference just told the truth. There's nothing you can do about that because the truth is an absolute defense." (There's that phrase again.)

Here's a worst-case scenario: Some lawyer does file suit against you for, in effect, being honest. Who will win? You will! And more than likely, all the attorneys' fees will have to be paid by the person who sued you, so you'll be out nothing. You simply told the truth.

## SHOULD YOU EVER OFFER AN OPINION OR JUST STICK WITH FACTS?

Some companies stick to a "just the facts" policy, but if you've agreed to serve as a reference, that will be practically impossible to do.

For instance, suppose a prospective employer calls and asks you how you'd describe so-and-so's interpersonal skills. How can you avoid interjecting your opinion into your response? You really can't, and there's nothing wrong with that—as long as what you say is an *honestly* held opinion. To the reader, the word *honest* must seem to appear repeatedly in the text of this book. Well, you're right; it *does*. There is a simple reason for that. Honesty is the *key* to the entire process of reference checking. Nevertheless, if job seekers were always honest to a fault, there *still* would be a need for reference checking because the ultimate reason for the exercise is to ensure the skills, experience, and training of the candidate match the requirements of the job. So, even in a perfectly honest world, reference checking would still be an invaluable tool in the process of hiring people.

Just sticking to a recitation of facts is not going to accomplish the objective of ensuring a solid job match. Honestly held opinions are vital to effective reference checking and, as a practical matter, shouldn't be avoided. "How do you think so-and-so will be able to handle the task of successfully carrying out X?" The only possible way to answer that question is to offer your opinion. You don't actually "know" the correct answer as a fact. Now, your opinion can be *based* on facts—like how well the job seeker has handled the same or similar tasks in the *past*, but the *future* (of course) is an unknown. An element of opinion cannot be avoided.

Although the range of possible responses to that question is very wide, one of your options might be, "Based on my observation of so-and-so doing exactly the same task under my supervision before, I'm sure he/she will be able to successfully do that for your company." Another response might be, "Although so-and-so was never asked to do X while I worked for him/her, I'm sure he/she could easily handle it because . . ." Are there elements of subjective opinion in either of those two theoretical responses? Of course there are.

Keep in mind, also, that a wise employer isn't going to talk to one reference alone, but usually three. If all three references share the same views about things like management style or interpersonal skills or career development needs, then the prospective employer will have all the validation required to make the sort of informed employment decision that will lead to a good match of candidate and job requirements, not just in terms of how the candidate fits the requirements, but also what the candidate may need to continue his or her professional growth and thereby become even more valuable to the employer. And that, after all, is still the point of the whole exercise.

# IS WHAT YOU SAY A REFLECTION ON YOUR COMPANY?

Many employers seem to hold fast to the preceding belief. That's one of the motivations behind the popular adoption of no-comment policies. There are attorneys who specialize in employment law who also seem to agree. That said, let's look at why this area of reference checking provokes such a sensitive response.

This happens to be the point at which facts and opinions part company. Facts are essentially things such as start dates, job titles, and ending dates. There's very little risk involved in a former employer providing that kind of factual information.

Opinion, on the other hand, can be misconstrued as representing an "official" view held by the former employer and, therefore, might expose the company to potential lawsuits based on the opinions offered by its employees. That's precisely why it's so important for you, as a potential reference, to make it *perfectly clear* that you are not speaking on behalf of the company when discussing someone's past job performance. You are merely offering your honestly held opinion.

In the course of a reference interview, suppose you offer the opinion that the job seeker for whom you've agreed to be a reference needs more training to be able to successfully accomplish task X. Also, suppose that as a result, the job seeker isn't hired. Are you and your company running the risk of being sued? Potentially, yes. But there are other factors to consider. Suppose the other references with whom the prospective employer spoke *all* agreed that, to do task X, the candidate will need more training. If you've made it clear that you're only expressing your own opinion and that what you have to say should not be construed as representing any company-held view, you should feel secure. As long as you've offered an honestly held opinion, it's highly unlikely the job seeker will prevail if you and your company are sued. Remember that part about the truth being an absolute defense? That's why neither you nor your company should fear the prospect of litigation under the circumstances just described.

Let's flip this example around. Suppose, in your zeal to be helpful to your friend who has asked you to serve as a reference, you *overstate* what she can do. Let's also suppose that based on your exaggeration, the candidate is hired and fails miserably at the job. Or, worse yet, let's imagine that because you overstated her ability, other employees are somehow injured because of the candidate's incompetence. Do you think the new employer might sue you for saying the candidate was capable of handling a task you *knew* she could not? You would be vulnerable to litigation, and what's more, that employer probably could win. Why? Because the opinion you offered, although laudatory, was not honestly held. So, as we've noted, being less than honest in either direction—exaggerating or sabotaging—is taking a foolish and unnecessary risk.

We've come full circle, then, all the way back to the importance of honesty.

In this chapter, we've discussed how to make sure calls made to you, as a reference, are legitimate, how to deal with company policy, the types of questions you should and shouldn't answer, and how to respond to such questions. We've also discussed the critical importance of being honest when answering questions, the importance of expressing your opinion, and the difference between speaking for yourself and speaking on behalf of your company. Refer to Chapter 13 for more information on the practical implementation of a reference-giving policy at your workplace.

The central message of this chapter is the important role you have to play when asked to serve as a reference for a friend and coworker. By following the simple commonsense guidelines in this chapter, you can play a pivotal role in helping your friends not only get the job for which they're best qualified, but also helping avoid job mismatches, which always leads to one kind of grief or another.

# CHAPTER 12

# THE ETHICS OF CHECKING REFERENCES

## IS REFERENCE CHECKING A STANDARD BUSINESS PRACTICE?

Yes. Reference checking always has been and always will be a standard business practice. How else can the employer find out if the candidate is all he or she claims to be? Not only that, but of equal importance is whether or not the candidate can do all that he or she claims.

Let's now take a serious look at the way many employers have carried out the employee selection process. In an earlier time, most people were hired on the basis of just two, and sometimes three, criteria:

+ The contents of their résumé

+ A job interview

+ Occasionally (but not always) a letter of introduction written by a trusted friend or relative

Prior to the industrial revolution, some combination of these three criteria were all the typical shopkeeper or craftsperson needed in order to make a hiring decision. Why? Because before the days of industrialization, there were no large companies that employed hundreds, let alone thousands, of employees. Most businesses were very small operations, particularly during the colonial period in this country. The owner usually worked right alongside the handful of people he or she employed and could readily see if they were doing the job or not. If they weren't performing up to expected standards, such employees were usually "discharged" and they went right on to some other job. Except for the true craftsperson or artisan, most employees were unskilled laborers who worked as apprentices or were indentured to the business owner. There were no laws protecting workers' rights. The employee either measured up to the requirements of the job or he didn't. Period. (And incidentally, outside the domestic realm, it *was* almost always a "he.")

Because most job seekers were unskilled, not to mention uneducated, drifting from one job to another was not uncommon at all. So there was little need to find out if the job seeker really was whom he or she claimed to be or could do the job required. The person either learned the job quickly or was replaced. With the exception of a few colleges that focused on offering a classical education, there were no such things as trade schools or business schools. The willingness to work long and hard hours was the best test of someone's employability.

Since the industrial revolution, however, and the advent of mass production, job specialization has been constantly increasing as the skills required to do very specialized jobs have become more and more demanding. As the requirements of jobs became more specialized, it became increasingly more important to hire people who already had the experience, skills, and training to handle those specialized jobs. Gone were the days of having the time to learn the skills required to do a job as an apprentice to a skilled artisan. The pace of business had increased to such an extent that job knowledge became a prerequisite, not a luxury.

Another factor that made reference checking more common was the introduction of mass communication and the advent of a mobile workforce. Even during the last half of the nineteenth century, most job seekers never ventured very far from home. Most stayed on the family farm or worked in a family business. It was more or less expected that young people would take jobs in their hometowns and stay there. Since the early part of the twentieth century, however, the face of the job market has changed dramatically, particularly during the period between World War I and the end of World War II.

Reference checking, evolving as something more than a casual conversation between store owners in the same town, started becoming a necessity during the post–World War II era. In the late 1940s, reference checking slowly outgrew the casual conversation stage and developed into a structured interview process requiring considerable skill, training, intuition, and good judgment. Since the 1980s, reference checking, in one form or another, has become more of an art than a perfunctory checklist of yes/no questions sometimes posed to previous employers.

It has been only within the last decade or so that many hiring managers realized that just having an "honest face" might not be sufficient information for basing a hiring decision. That's especially alarming in light of all the increasingly specialized jobs that have been created in the high-paid, fast-paced, increasingly computerized business world of today. The point, I think, is that serious reference checking, as a stand-alone specialty service, is relatively new. But the basic process of one employer talking to another about how a young person might work out as a clerk in the local dry goods store has been going on, informally, for at least the last hundred years in this country.

## DOES IT MAKE SENSE FOR PROSPECTIVE AND FORMER EMPLOYERS TO SHARE INFORMATION?

The more important version of this question, perhaps, should be, "Why *doesn't* it make sense?" Since we know that some people's best skill is interviewing, and that others are willing to embellish their résumés and claim academic achievements never earned, how else is a prospective employer supposed to objectively and subjectively evaluate a candidate for employment? Believe it or not, I have encountered employers who still think they can judge a candidate's prospects for job success solely on the basis of a face-to-face interview—and nothing more. Clearly, this attitude is a holdover from the show-me-an-honest-face mentality that was in fashion generations ago—and still evident as recently as the 1980s. For jobs that almost anybody could perform with only a few hours of training, an honest face still gets some people hired, but that simplistic approach to hiring is rapidly disappearing from the employment process. Of course, it makes sense for prospective and former employers to be able to share information; the only sensible limitation on that sort of sharing is that the information should be always true and accurate. And that's where the job seeker comes into the picture.

Because we've become such a litigious society—negligent hiring, negligent referral, defamation of character, invasion of privacy—threats of all these civil actions have worked together to create something of a hostile environment for the employer. The employer's ability to share information about employees has become clouded and confused to such an extent that employers, who should know better, have begun to wonder if they're legally allowed to share information with each other at all. Let me be perfectly clear about this: Yes, they are.

Unequivocally, employers *are* allowed to share information, and more importantly, it makes excellent sense that they should be allowed to do so.

To suggest that they aren't makes no sense at all, except to the prospective employee with something to hide. And within the framework of information sharing, the job seeker becomes the facilitator who makes it happen and who, frankly, should want to make it happen—not for the employer's sake, but for his or her own. After all, he or she is the person who wants to become employed.

## HOW ELSE ARE YOU GOING TO FIND OUT WHO'S RIGHT FOR THE JOB OR WHO WILL BE A RESPONSIBLE TENANT?

How, indeed? A great deal can be learned about a candidate's *technical* skills through a job interview with someone whose technical skills are within the same field (or at the very least, closely related). It would be naïve to suggest that a highly trained organic chemist couldn't get a fair sense of a candidate's knowledge of organic chemistry through a one-on-one interview process. What is much more difficult to determine, however, is how capable the candidate will be in terms of soft skills, like working well with others. It's more difficult to know how effectively the candidate's management style will fit within an organization's existing corporate culture, or a hundred other things that are outside the scope of technical skills.

For people screening possible renters, the challenge is even greater. Within the process of tenant selection, the range of available expertise is, by definition, very limited. Obviously, things like job skills don't really matter when you're considering someone who wants to rent space from you. Personal references are a waste of time. Face-to-face interviews are useful, but, again, there are people very adept at selling themselves who couldn't take care of a cardboard box if their life depended on it. The only way to evaluate a prospective tenant is to talk to other landlords from whom the prospective tenant has rented in the past. For prospective tenants who've only rented, perhaps, from one other landlord, a credit check is probably the only other way to get a useful sense of financial responsibility.

You may recall from an earlier chapter the example of the sound and vibration engineer who was technically proficient but who couldn't get along with anybody. Short of careful reference checking, how else could that tendency have been uncovered? Is it likely that during the job interview the engineer would have admitted, "Yes, I'm very technically competent, but I have a very abrasive personality and I tend to offend people with whom I work"? Of course not. Would a credit check or court check have revealed the personality problem? Would a paper-and-pencil test have revealed the extent to which this engineer tended to annoy others? Maybe. It's far more likely, in my view, that most personality assessment instruments would have indicated a strong personality or a tendency to be a perfectionist. These kinds of tools are relatively ineffective at revealing how his personality would impact his relationship with others. I suggest the only way to determine this individual's difficulty getting along with others (which even *he* didn't realize) would be through careful reference checking.

The problem area, here again, was not with his technical skill or ability, but with his soft skills—in this case, how others reacted to his abrasive personality.

The point of all this is to make it very clear there is really no other way to discover who's right for the job or who will be a good tenant besides careful reference checking. And to the extent that you have something the job seeker or prospective tenant wants, you have control over the process. You get to decide how much or how little you intend to do to make sure you're hiring the best people or renting to the best-possible tenants.

By the same token, I would never disparage any of the other pre-employment tools that are available. They all have value, but standing alone, none of them will give you the insight you should have when making important hiring or renter decisions. I have said before and continue to stand by my belief that the up-front investment required to make as sure as possible that you're finding the right people is a sound business decision. Being confident the most qualified people are being hired and that the most responsible tenants are signing leases costs pocket change compared to the cost of doing less and making a hiring or leasing mistake. The more information you have about people in a work setting or as prospective renters, the better.

There are occasions where employers become desperate to fill an important job vacancy or where a landlord needs a warm body to fill an apartment. But that's never an excuse, in my view, to ignore the reference-checking step in the selection process. I've heard employers, in particular, say they just "couldn't afford" to let a qualified candidate get away, so they hired the person essentially on the spot— before the candidate took a job somewhere else. But as we've said before, the price of careful reference checking is nothing compared to the cost of a hiring mistake.

## A COMMONSENSE APPROACH: INVOLVING THE CANDIDATE

One of the major concerns job seekers have is their fear of what references might say about them. That fear is usually founded on some basically false beliefs:

- Prospective employers will be calling supervisors with whom they didn't particularly get along.

171

* A former boss will intentionally sabotage their job chances through some perverse desire for revenge.

* Someone with only a limited knowledge of their overall performance will not provide an accurate description of just how well they really did their job.

All these applicant fears can be minimized *if* the prospective employer defines the parameters of the reference-checking process.

On the other side of the table is the fear by employers that if they ask the candidate to provide work-related references, the references will somehow or other be coached to just say good things about the candidate. Here's how the song goes:

"Well, if we ask candidates to provide the references, they'll just give us a list of people who'll say they did a great job."

Maybe. It really depends on the skill of the person doing the checking. If employers and landlords simply embrace the concept that the job seeker or the prospective tenant has an important role to play in the process, both sides of the equation balance out.

The prospective employer has every right to specify the *types* of references desired from the candidate. Doing so actually eliminates most of the trepidation on the part of the job seeker who is worried about what references will say. Remember, the job seeker—within employer-defined limits—gets to choose his or her references.

Let the candidates or prospective renters pick their references, as defined by you, but then make sure you're asking *the right questions*. That's where the art of reference checking comes in to play. And that's essentially what this book is about.

Even if references only *want* to say good things, that's pretty hard to do when you ask open-ended questions. For example, one open-ended question that could be asked is, "How would you describe so-and-so's management style?" or "What does so-and-so need to do to continue his/her own professional growth?"

So, simply involving the job seeker or prospective tenant in the process reduces the trepidation on both sides of the equation and defuses the old bias against reference checking.

## THE CURRENT STATE OF THE SELECTION PROCESS

What is the current state of things in the employee and tenant selection process? Sure, there's still a vast sea of misunderstanding about what can and can't be done in reference checking. But in my view, that's more of a *reactive* situation than an actual status report. As an employer or a landlord, you can choose to take a *proactive* approach. I also think the business climate is changing. The horrible events of 9/11/01 have made both employers and landlords keenly aware of the need to know more about the people they're hiring or to whom they're renting. But a huge void still exists in terms of any practical understanding of what can and can't be done through careful reference checking.

Throughout this book, I've tried to make the case for more, rather than less, reference and background checking. My main concern at this point is that too many readers will still see the exercise as some sort of intrusion on the careers and lives of those who've made a mistake or two along the way. To an extent, that may be true, but the reality of the situation is that we *all* have to be responsible for our own actions and suffer the consequences of those actions.

On the other hand, reference checking should never be viewed in a vacuum. That's why discussing it is so important. The essential truth behind thorough reference checking is to evaluate job performance *over time*. The same is true for renters. What kind of tenants have these people been *over time?* It's not the one-time mistake that ruins an otherwise promising career. It's not the one misunderstanding with a landlord that paints the entire portrait of the prospective renter. It's the *record* of responsibility *over time* that illuminates useful information—saving everyone time, hurtful misunderstandings, and money.

There's an old legalism that says something like "every dog is entitled to one free bite." That may or may not be true. But the everyday meaning of that phrase is simply that we *all* make mistakes in our lives. If we learn from those mistakes and become better people because of it, we're better off. Most people do learn from their isolated mistakes as employees or renters. The same is true of employers and landlords. One of the things real reference checking does best is demonstrate what a job seeker or renter has done with the knowledge learned from an isolated error in judgment. It's the job seeker or prospective renter who hasn't learned by his or her mistakes that employers and landlords are trying to avoid.

The bottom line is this: Employers and landlords need to be more proactive in the employee and renter selection process. The choice to do so is freely yours.

In this chapter we've discussed reference checking within a historical context as a standard business practice. We've talked about the value gained from employers sharing information, and along with that, we've asked how else employers and landlords can make the best hiring and renting decisions possible. We've looked at the standard no-comment policy from the standpoint of the employee and the prospective employer, and we've talked about the common sense of involving the candidate and renter in the reference-checking process. Finally, we've talked about the general public's attitudes toward reference checking—from a philosophical point of view. At this juncture, there should be no question about the legality, benefit, or practicality of reference checking. If doubt persists, go back and review this book again. It's all there.

# CHAPTER 13

# IMPLEMENTING A REFERENCE-CHECKING PROGRAM

## GETTING REFERENCES

Every organization operates differently, ranging from its basic mission statement to who's responsible for buying paper clips. HR departments are even more diverse in their approach to the hiring function (as you may recall from the beginning of this book, there isn't even a communality regarding the meaning of terms used in the pre-employment process).

There's no question that establishing a consistent reference and background-checking policy is a very important thing to do. That's exactly what this chapter is designed to do—give you a blueprint to follow so that you can implement a reference-checking program within your own organization. Exactly how much preparatory work needs to be done will depend on the size of your organization. For very small companies with only one location, the process should be easy. For larger operations with multiple facilities and locations, the process is no less easy, but could be more time-consuming. Regardless of the size of the organization, however, the basic principle to remember is that more information is always better than less when it comes to hiring people. Accepting this notion is the starting point for developing a program to accomplish the goal of effective reference checking.

Part of this chapter is devoted to putting in place a program to check the references of incoming candidates for employment. Another part shows you how your departing employees can list current employees as references who, by approved company policy, are permitted to talk to prospective employees.

As we've discussed, you should strongly consider instituting a policy that, within limits, allows your employees to comment about former employees—because they're doing it anyway! Having a program and policy in place simply acknowledges what's already happening, and it makes good legal sense, too. Having such a policy in writing will practically eliminate any potential liability for your company.

## Small Companies

For companies with only one location and not very many employees— from a handful to a few hundred—establishing a reference-checking program should be a relatively straightforward exercise. It's simply a matter of stating, by policy, that reference checking will be part of the preemployment process for every new hire and that no job offer can be made—by anyone—until the reference report and any appropriate background checks have been completed and reviewed by whomever is responsible for hiring people or authorizing that a job offer be made. In other words, even if functional managers have hiring authority, there should still be one person responsible for making sure all pre-job-offer steps have been completed and reviewed *first*, before authorizing that a job offer can be made.

Hiring authority within a small company should be centralized, if possible. Only one person should have the authority to make job offers or to approve, beforehand, the job offers to be made by others. While the final authority to make the offer should rest with one person, input from the functional manager to whom the candidate will report is also essential. That does not mean, however, that the functional manager should have independent hiring authority. Nor does it mean that the functional manager should do the reference checking. At least one degree of separation is desirable to ensure objectivity.

In a small company, the HR manager should discuss the responsibilities particular to the job with the functional manager, so that the questions asked of references can be tailored to address them. It also makes good sense for the HR manager to check the prime candidate's references *before* conducting a face-to-face interview to, again, help ensure objectivity, but also to be able to use the input from references to help guide the interview. Then, if there are other highly technical matters to be discussed, they should be addressed during the second interview with the functional manager to whom the candidate will report.

Prospective employees should be told, prior to any offer of employment, that it's the company's policy to check references and to conduct whatever other background checks are deemed appropriate under the circumstances. Every applicant should be asked to sign a comprehensive waiver granting the prospective employer or its agents express permission to contact references or anyone else familiar with the candidate's work history or job performance. (See the waiver in Chapter 4.) Every candidate should be asked to fill out a reference information form listing specific types of references, such as former superiors, peers, and subordinates. Remember, it won't always be possible to come up with that particular mix, but references should at least be people with whom the candidate has worked on a daily basis for a minimum of six months within the last five to seven years. It's perfectly fine to specify those parameters to job applicants. It should also be up to the candidate to supply complete and accurate contact information to enable you to easily contact those references.

Here, again, are the steps:

1. Review the applications and conduct any other appropriate background checks to ensure the candidate is who he or she claims to be. (See Chapter 7 for more information on the various background checks and how to do them.) Then do the initial interviews.

2. Conduct a thorough job performance-based reference check on the top one or two candidates.

3. After those reports have been carefully examined and reviewed, conduct an in-depth interview, which can include addressing any concerns contained in the reference report.

4. Hold a final interview, including in the process the functional manager to whom the candidate will report.

5. Then make the final hiring decision.

One optional approach would be to carry out all the preceding preemployment steps, including the follow-up interview of the top candidate—and *then* conduct a thorough reference check as the final step in the process before making an offer of employment. My preference, however, is to use the reference report as a guide for conducting the final interview.

As a practical matter, however, the actual reference-checking exercise should not be done until the final candidates have been identified and interviewed at least once, and all the other preemployment steps have been taken. But, as we've noted before, you should not tell the candidate that a job offer is contingent on the outcome of the reference checks.

While the processes outlined here can be modified to fit individual companies, the basics that every small business should absolutely follow are these:

* By policy, establish that no job offer can be made until references are thoroughly checked.

* Establish the rule that every candidate must sign a comprehensive waiver granting express permission to the employer or its agents to contact references.

* Be sure that candidates are required to provide specific types of references.

* Make it a policy that no job offer can be made *contingent* upon reference checking.

## Individual Employers and Landlords

Regardless of whether you're hiring a contractor, health care provider, tutor, looking for a new dentist, or renting property, the fundamentals remain essentially the same. Unlike a small corporation, however, you're your own HR department, which means that the only piece you probably can't incorporate into the process is delegating the reference checking to someone else. You'll have to do it all, but the steps are the same as those outlined previously:

1. Solicit applications and verify the information provided.

2. Set up face-to-face interviews with whomever appears to be best suited for the position or the most desirable renter.

3. Carefully check references.

4. Make a hiring/rental decision.

## *Large Companies*

For purposes of this book, large companies can be defined as those with multiple locations, other subsidiary business units, or businesses with multiple functional areas that operate with considerable autonomy contained in at least one large complex.

Before a reference-checking program can effectively be put into place, the first step in the process should be to conduct a preemployment audit to determine what sorts of reference-checking, background-checking, and other screening techniques are already actually in place. This is another example of theory and practice not necessarily being exactly the same. For instance, I recall one employer who used an outside recruiting firm to identify, screen, and initially interview candidates for employment. They were also supposed to contact two references. Once the recruiter had presented the top candidate to the prospective employer, the functional manager—not anyone in HR—was supposed to contact two more references and also carry out another face-to-face interview. That was what was *supposed* to happen.

The mere size of an organization can create process consistency problems. In many instances, for example, the simple fact that various business units may be scattered across several states makes it difficult to ensure that each and every step in the process is followed. Large corporations, particularly ones that contain business units that have been acquired, by nature tend toward individualism, because they're used to doing things the way they did before acquisition, which makes the implementation of process consistency more difficult. Further complicating the situation is the tendency by corporate to allow separate business units to maintain some autonomy that, by definition, tends to discourage process consistency in the identification, evaluation, and selection of new employees.

During the course of the preemployment audit referred to earlier, the question was asked, "Your policy states that the functional manager is to contact two additional references before making a hiring decision. How often does that really happen?"

The response? "Less than half of the time."

"Why?"

"Well, our functional managers get busy doing other things, and not all of them really know how to check references, so those additional references aren't always called."

In this particular situation, the people in HR acknowledged that company policy wasn't being followed, *and* they admitted they didn't know what sorts of questions were being asked, if other functional managers were asking the same or different questions, or whether hiring decisions were being based on questions that shouldn't have been asked in the first place! How scary is that?

One of the reasons that every business, large or small, should have a *standard* preemployment and reference-checking program is to ensure process consistency. And that consistency should extend throughout the organization, no matter how many locations it has, no matter how many subsidiary companies there are, and no matter how many people within a large complex have some degree of hiring authority. The potential liability to which the company is exposing itself is staggering. Why? Inconsistent hiring practices could easily lead to charges of discrimination or wrongful denial of employment, or to an accusation of unfair hiring practices. Rather than face all that, it simply makes good business sense—let alone *legal* sense—to ensure that process consistency exists throughout the corporation.

Once the company audit phase is complete and an evaluation of the overall employment process has been done, the next step is to adopt a corporatewide policy with regard to the employment process, including reference checking. The steps in the hiring process should be carefully outlined and set in concrete to guarantee every prospective employee is treated exactly the same—and that obviously includes the reference-checking process. Part of the corporate policy should contain a statement saying something like, "No offer of employment may be made until a job-performance-based reference report has been conducted and reviewed by ( *HR department or HR position title* ).

Here's an example of how one company does it. They have, by policy, told all their domestic operations that no job offer can be made until references have been checked, a copy of every reference report has been sent to the corporate human resources department, and approval has been returned to authorize the extension of an offer of employment. The reason behind their decision was to not only ensure process consistency, but to make sure that local hiring managers weren't missing or ignoring red flags contained in the reference report. As an aside, by approaching their hiring decisions in this way, turnover was significantly reduced and the cost-per-hire went down dramatically. And that bottom line, of course, is the *fiscal point* of reference checking.

Another reason this approach was adopted was so the corporate HR department could regain some control over the hiring process, not just for the sake of control, but for the purpose of *knowing* who was being hired and ensuring that the hiring processes were legally consistent in all their domestic facilities.

The next step in the process of implementing a reference-checking program is to develop a standardized waiver for every job applicant to sign. Part of the preemployment package also should include a reference information sheet for each candidate to fill out as part of the actual job application ducument. So, in one document, not only are references requested, but also work history and other pertinent information obtained.

The candidate background-checking process will undoubtedly vary from company to company. Some employers require drug testing; others don't. Some require court checks; others don't. Actually, the list of background-checking options is almost endless. But the point of this particular exercise, as we have noted before, is to make sure that the candidate is who he or she claims to be and that the basic information on the job application is, in fact, true.

Once likely prospects have been identified, the initial interview by the hiring manager should follow. For those job seekers still in the running after the initial job interviews, the next step should be careful reference checking. It's important to note at this point that neither the hiring manager nor the functional manager (the person with a vacancy to fill) should be doing the reference checking. To be most effective, reference checking should be done, ideally, by someone who is "independent" of the process—that is, someone who doesn't know the candidate, has never seen nor talked to him or her, and who can be totally objective when speaking with references. If it isn't possible to have someone responsible for handing all the reference checking within the HR function, references should be checked by the hiring manager before the face-to-face interview takes place. It goes without saying that all of us, even the most experienced hiring manager, cannot help but form subliminal opinions about the candidate through the interview process. Total objectivity should be the watchword for whomever is assigned the task of reference checking.

For functional managers who may be reading this book, I can already hear the complaint, "But I've got a spot to fill! I can't wait for all this nonsense to go on. I need somebody in that job now!"

Well, that may be so, but it's far better to take a few extra days to be safe than to rush into a hiring decision you'll regret down the road. As we've seen, inappropriate hiring decisions can be very expensive, not just in terms of the cost of replacing that person, but also in terms of disrupting operations and damaging employee morale. Never lose sight of the fact that there are always practical and monetary costs associated with every hiring mismatch.

Put as simply as possible, no job offer should be made until references have been contacted and their comments evaluated by someone at least one step removed from the other steps in the process.

Once that's done, assuming the candidate's past job performance fits the requirements of the job, then a job offer can be authorized. Reference checking should be an institutionalized part of the pre-employment process. It should be seen not only as a sensible business practice, but also as a strict company (or corporate) policy. It is just as important as finding out if the candidate has falsified something on his or her résumé or job application.

## GIVING REFERENCES

For many employers the whole notion of allowing their employees to serve as references for former employees may sound like heresy. The no-comment concept is so deeply entrenched in the corporate mentality of many HR people that even the slightest suggestion that it is possible to allow employees to serve as references is rejected out of hand.

The key to remember, however, is that the benefits of reference checking pay as valuable dividends to you, the employer, at the end of someone's employment with your company as they do at the beginning. When you, the prospective employer, ask job seekers to sign a waiver allowing you to talk to the candidate's references, that's one side of a valuable coin. Asking departing employees to sign a waiver allowing current employees to talk to the next prospective employer is simply the other side of the same coin.

If a departing employee wants to list one or more of your current employees as references—and those employees have indicated they are willing to serve as references for the departing employee—all you need to do is have the departing employee sign the new waiver (see Chapter 10). This relieves you, the employer, from incurring liability for what they say, as long as they are specifically told three things:

+ To only respond to questions that have to do with job performance
+ That they only offer honestly held opinions
+ To state only documented facts

Other suggestions to this new approach include keeping a copy of each signed waiver in the departing employee's permanent personnel file—once the policy regarding serving as references is established. Then, make sure every employee has a copy of it and understands the waiver's meaning.

The object of this is to give you, the employer, another layer of protection from potential liability acknowledging (as we've already noted), a practice that most likely is already taking place. By acknowledging it, and adding an extra layer of protection, you're getting the same level of insulation at the end of the employment experience as you want at the beginning.

There's another factor to consider: You, as an employer, should *want* to see good employees advance their careers. If an employee has performed well, there is absolutely no reason *not* to let prospective employers know about it be aware of the quality of that performance while working for your organization.

If a departing candidate does not want to sign the waiver allowing your employees to speak to a prospective employer, for whatever reason, then just go right back to your no-comment policy regarding that employee. One would think, however, that *not* wanting former coworkers to serve as references would raise a major red flag for the prospective employer.

If, on the other hand, the departing employee wants to ask former employees of yours to serve as references, you have nothing to worry about at all. No matter what they say about the departing employee, you couldn't possibly be at risk.

This whole notion of *giving* as well as *getting* references is consistent with the idea that people who have performed well should be able to ask coworkers to say so. By the same token, enabling current employees to state facts or give honestly held opinions *could* help another employer avoid making an inappropriate and costly hiring mistake.

In this chapter we've looked at ways for both small and large employers to institute a reference-checking program as part of their hiring process. We've looked at the importance of process consistency, and we've considered some of the reasons why it makes good sense to establish, by policy, a reference-checking program that takes place before any offer of employment is made. Most importantly, we've explored the new field of why an employer should allow employees to serve as references for former employees—and how to do it while enabling that employer to have an extra layer of protection against liability.

Finally, we looked at the good business sense that underlies the notion of employers being able to truthfully share job performance information in both directions: when they're trying to hire good people and also when good people decide to move on.

Clearly, there's no question about the fact that every company should have a reference-checking program in place. Historically, careful reference checking has been the missing piece in the employment process puzzle. Putting such a program in place isn't that difficult, nor is it expensive. It may change the traditional, time-honored way many employees have been hired in the past, but it will surely improve the quality (and associated economics) of new hires in the future.

# CHAPTER 14

# AFTER THE PERSON IS HIRED

## REFERENCES FOR INTERNAL PROMOTION

Reference checking has another application that employers can utilize. A carefully prepared reference report can be used as an internal screening tool to assist in finding the best candidate for promotion or reassignment *from within* the organization. As a matter of policy, many employers already promote from within before ever going outside the organization to hire someone new. It's a sensible and economical thing to do, particularly in larger organizations where the talent pool is a little deeper and current employees are, in most respects, known quantities. Many jobs are simply posted within the organization, and current employees who feel they have the qualifications for the opening may apply for them. It's a very common practice.

So, how does reference checking apply in situations like these? The process is even more straightforward and uncomplicated than it would be when hiring someone entirely new to the organization.

The process is essentially the same. As an employer, all you have to do is adopt a policy whereby all employees are made aware of the fact that in-house references are needed as part of the response to every internal job posting.

Doing a reference report on an internal candidate is the purest and, in many respects, most understandable way to grasp the value of and the justification for the exercise. Clearly, the goal is to make the best-possible hiring decision for the job to be filled. What else could its purpose be? Furthermore, promoting or reassigning an internal candidate should eliminate the need for additional ancillary checks, unless there's some reason to believe some unseen problem exists that could affect future job performance.

Here are just a few of the advantages associated with doing a reference check on an internal candidate:

♦ The individual is already an employee of the company. Therefore, no waiver would be required to discuss job performance with the individual's superiors, peers, or subordinates, unless an outside agency is used. In such a case, it would merely require that an authorization form be signed to allow references to be contacted.

♦ People asked to serve as references for the person seeking the promotion or reassignment wouldn't have to be concerned about any no-comment company policy, since it's totally an internal exercise. The comments made by references, in other words, would *not* be leaving the company. There's no need to be worried about the propriety of offering up honestly held opinions or stating documented facts in an internal reference-checking exercise.

♦ There would be no question about the legitimacy of the caller or the purpose of the call. What could be more straightforward than someone within the HR department of the XYZ Company talking with other employees of the XYZ Company? So, coworkers, superiors, or subordinates asked to serve as references would not only know the purpose of the call, they would also feel more at ease responding to reference questions. Actually, when you think about it, this exercise isn't all that different, conceptually, than an ordinary performance review during which input is sought from supervisors to construct the actual performance evaluation.

♦ It would be much easier for people seeking the promotion or reassignment to provide the names of appropriate people to serve as their references, since everyone involved with the process already understands exactly why it is being done. Here's how the dialogue could go:

"Hey, boss, there's an opening for a senior accountant over at Plant 5. I think I could handle the job, and it would mean a pay increase for me. Would you agree to be one of my references? May I give your name to HR as a contact about my work?"

♦ Offering promotions or reassignments to current employees usually means that the individual is very familiar with the company and its mode of operation. This definitely flattens out the learning curve that new employees always must overcome. This always makes in-house promotions and transfers simpler to execute.

♦ Lastly, the integrity of the exercise would be increased because there would be a higher level of accountability from references, since everyone involved in the process would know who was being contacted.

That doesn't guarantee, however, that everything will always be sweetness and light. Making sure the internal candidate is the right person for the job is just as important as it would be in the careful evaluation of an outside candidate. It's just a little easier to carry out when it's someone who's already on board.

The only twist that could conceivably be put on this process is if the current boss doesn't want to lose the internal candidate from his or her own department. In this event, HR would call the boss and discuss the prospect of moving the individual to another job within the company. It's possible the reassignment could be denied if it is critical that the individual remain in the position he or she currently holds. Most responsible companies, however, won't deny an internal promotion or reassignment to an otherwise qualified employee. It's good for morale, it's good for the organization, and the position being vacated can itself be filled from within or by someone new from the outside.

## Steps to Take for an Internal Reference Check

Because internal reference checking is a very up-front exercise, the basics remain the same. When the internal reference-checking policy is made known to all employees, none of it comes as a surprise to anyone. The goal of the exercise is still the same: to evaluate past job performance, to see how the internal candidate's skill sets and core competencies fit the requirements of the job, and to determine what the internal candidate may need to continue his or her own career development. Here's a quick checklist of how it should work:

♦ The internal candidate, assuming he or she meets the posted threshold requirements for the job, should be asked to provide the name of his or her immediate superior, as well as the name of a peer and a subordinate (if applicable). If the candidate doesn't have anyone working under his or her supervision, another coworker or former internal supervisor will do equally well. If the immediate supervisor hasn't known the internal candidate long enough to offer a valid assessment, previous supervisors can certainly be utilized, just as in an outside reference-checking situation. The point remains the same; references should be people with whom the candidate has worked on a daily basis within the last five to seven years.

- The internal candidate should ask the appropriate people to serve as references and fully explain what the situation is (assuming that, for some reason, they're not aware of the company's internal reference-checking policy), and then tell them to expect a call from HR. Furthermore, the internal candidate should also make a point of telling his or her references to *please* only provide honest responses to any questions that are asked and not to understate or overinflate any response regarding job performance. This simple, but important, request relieves stress for everyone involved.

- Someone within the HR function should be assigned the task of performing all reference checks for the organization. Whoever is selected should be trained to carefully and objectively carry out the reference-checking exercise. The task should *not* be delegated to a clerical person or someone unfamiliar with the steps of checking references thoroughly. More importantly, the task of reference checking should *not* be looked upon as a perfunctory task simply because it's an internal hire. Ensuring the right internal person fills the position is just as important as making the best-possible hiring decisions from among outside candidates. In many organizations, the internal promotion/reassignment exercise is often viewed as nothing more than a matter of filling out a few forms and making the change. How seriously the exercise is viewed will depend on the attitude of senior HR leadership. If they fail to see it as a critically important exercise, those responsible for carrying it out will not see it as important either.

- A minimum of three references should be contacted, and the entire list of standard questions should be asked (see Appendix A). The only variations will come at the end of the interview, and even at that, only the phraseology of the questions will change.

For example, when talking with references for inside candidates, the interviewer should slightly modify the question "Why do you think so-and-so is looking for other employment opportunities?" to "Why do you think so-and-so is interested in this promotion/ reassignment?" As another example, the question "Would you hire this person again?" becomes something like "Would you *recommend* this person for this promotion/ reassignment?"

• If more than one viable internal candidate has been identified, references should be checked on the top two or three candidates so the information contained in each reference report can be objectively evaluated. This includes a thorough comparison by the HR people, as well as the functional manager with the vacancy to fill.

  Once the information is collected and evaluated, a written recommendation should be made to the functional manager with the vacancy to fill. Armed with the information contained in the reference report, the functional manager should then have a face-to-face interview with those internal candidates who appear best suited to the job, to discuss not only the job requirements but also any areas of concern that may have come up during the reference-checking exercise.

• One last element needs to be taken into account when checking references on internal candidates. How do you inform the unsuccessful candidates they were not selected for the promotion or transfer? Clearly, they will assume that at least part of the reason they weren't selected was because of the comments made by their references. The best strategy is to honestly explain that after all factors were taken into consideration, it was felt that so-and-so was the person best suited for the job. There is no requirement to disclose who said what about any of the candidates, *but* the reference report *can* be a useful tool for an unsuccessful candidate in terms of providing guidance for professional or career growth. If this information can be shared in a constructive and noncritical manner, that input should be provided as a gesture of good faith.

## WHAT TO DO IF YOU GET BURNED

The whole point not only of careful reference checking but also of the entire preemployment process is to avoid getting burned by a bad hiring decision. In truth, if you follow the principles contained in this book, it really won't happen very often. To reduce your chances of getting burned, here are some additional tips:

- Before the reference-checking process begins, have a realistic sense of exactly what the requirements of the job will be—not just what the job description says, but what the job is really about.

  Think through what the corporate culture is like. The whole notion that a distinctive corporate culture even exists is looked upon with some skepticism by a few HR people. But identifying the corporate culture simply means doing some honest reflection on how things work within the organization, and looking at how "political" people orbit within it to get things done. This helps you make an objective assessment of the company's predominant leadership style and therefore make better hiring decisions.

- As part of the reference-checking exercise, specifically ask references for their opinions on how the candidate will fit into the job as it *really* is, not just how it's officially defined. Also ask how the candidate will fit into your corporate culture as you have observed it. There are questions specifically designed to address these particular issues (see Appendix A), which you should use toward the end of the interview.

♦ There is one other tip to keep in mind. While this book is about reference checking and its importance in the overall hiring process, checking references is not a guarantee of making foolproof hiring decisions. Reference checking is a piece of the process. Other key components of the hiring process should not be overlooked. Careful résumé review and job application screening, plus carefully structured job interviews, are all of equal importance.

Even if these tips are followed, there will still be the occasional job mismatch, in spite of everything you've done to avoid it. What can you do if that happens? First of all, use the reference report as a benchmark of what was said about the candidate and compare it to the problems that have come up since the job was offered and accepted. Compare the nature of the problems with any clues, that might be in the reference report, that were, perhaps, overlooked. Second, use the reference report as a guide for developing a plan for corrective action. Depending on how serious the mismatch is, the reference report may provide important clues that will give you the insight required to successfully address whatever the problem happens to be.

Most employers have clearly defined disciplinary procedures that are established by policy. Sometimes things just don't work out with a new employee, but the situation falls short of needing formal disciplinary action. There really are three steps to follow when it appears that a job mismatch may have occurred:

1. Talk about the issues with the employee. It's more likely than not there has been some sort of disconnection, misunderstanding,

or miscommunication about what was said regarding the employee's suitability for the job by his or her references. Sometimes the requirements of the job were misrepresented or wrongly perceived by the candidate. Look for clues. Talk to the new employee. Discuss what references had to say. In other words, make every effort to identify the problems and address them as soon as possible.

2. Another alternative is to move the individual to another job within the organization—if that's possible. Depending upon the clues that may be found in the reference report and the discussions you have with the employee, it may be mutually advantageous to move the person to another position within the organization that is a better fit. That won't always be possible within a small organization, but it's often quite possible within large corporations.

3. The last option, of course, is termination.

I recall an instance many years ago where we were asked to check references on a candidate for a marketing manager's position. All three references had consistently positive things to say about every aspect of the candidate's overall job performance over time. The candidate was hired and almost immediately began to experience difficulty. The problems that emerged had nothing to do with quality, but were the result of the increased volume of work that had to be done and the pace at which things moved within the hiring organization. In a nutshell, the person hired for the job simply could not keep up with the demands of the job. When we went back to look for clues that might have been contained in the comments by references, we noted a remark about how meticulous the candidate tended to be, in terms of attention to detail. Another reference talked about how deliberate the candidate was and how committed he was to going the extra mile to do the best job possible. A third reference noted that the only thing the candidate needed for career advancement was learning to manage more than one task at a time—to be able "to keep more than one ball in the air."

As isolated bits of information, none of these comments suggested the candidate could not handle a high-volume, fast-paced environment. Upon reflection, however, that should have emerged as a concern to the prospective employer—if not to us!

It was at that point, as a matter of fact, that we started paying significantly more attention to the value of understanding the nature of the job into which the candidate would be placed, as well as the nature of the corporate culture. The client did not mention, nor did we ask, if the environment was exceedingly fast-paced or that the volume of work to be done was unusually high. That's because the employer didn't *perceive* it that way. To them, the pace and the volume of work were perfectly normal. The result? An unintentional job mismatch. Could it have been avoided? Perhaps.

The point, of course, is that the more the prospective employer understands the culture of his organization—not just in theory but in practice—the less the likelihood of a job mismatch. In the foregoing example, upon reflection, there were definitely clues the candidate's prospects for success were slim. But neither the prospective employer nor we caught them. The result was a termination simply because the newly hired marketing manager simply could not keep up. In other environments the individual had performed well, and would again, but just not in this one. Did the experience hurt the person's subsequent job prospects? No, not really. The net effect was the candidate gained a much higher level of awareness of the type of organization for which he would be best suited, a place that required attention to detail and thoroughness. And it also highlighted the need for this person to learn to manage more than one project at a time.

It would be naïve to suggest that every job mismatch has a happy ending. Once in a great while, despite the best efforts of all those involved, a ringer will slip through and be hired. When the mistake is discovered, termination is usually the result, but without the tag line that reads "they all lived happily ever after."

The point of this entire book has been to reduce the possibility of getting burned—hiring someone who, for whatever reason, can't do the job. We know the costs, monetary and otherwise, of a hiring mistake. That's why, without exception, having more information about a job seeker is always better than having less.

If the principles outlined in this book are followed consistently, both in theory and in practice, and if they are looked upon as essential to the hiring process and become standard operating procedure in your organization, then better hiring decisions will be the rule. Hiring mismatches will be the rare exception.

It is through working with people we reach the vast majority of our goals. Whether it's ensuring the safety of a precious child placed in the care of a babysitter or hiring a new Fortune 500 CEO, people are the critical element in nearly every endeavor in life. Choosing the right ones, therefore, is essential. It is hoped this book, in some small way, will make finding the best people a little easier.

# SAMPLE QUESTIONS TO ASK WHEN CHECKING REFERENCES

*Note:* These questions can be phrased in any number of ways and, obviously, can be modified to fit particular situations or different positions. Generally speaking, I recommend that they be asked in this order, but the order can be changed, and occasionally, the reference will provide information about a particular area of concern before the question is asked.

## SAMPLE QUESTIONS FOR MANAGERS

1. How are you acquainted with (*name of candidate*)?
2. How long did you and he/she work together?
3. During that time, what was your job title? What was his/her job title?
4. What were his/her primary responsibilities on the job?
5. How would you describe the overall quality of his/her job performance?

6. How productive do you think he/she was on the job?

7. How would you describe his/her attitude on the job?

8. Did he/she have supervisory responsibilities? How would you describe his/her style/success as a supervisor?

9. What do you think his/her main strengths were on the job?

10. Were there any areas in which you thought he/she could have improved? Were there any areas of weakness or deficiency in his/her overall job performance, as you saw it?

11. How would you compare his/her overall job performance to that of others with whom you've worked doing essentially the same job?

12. What do you think motivates him/her to *want* to do a good job?

13. How would you describe his/her overall ability to work effectively with others in a work setting?

14. How would you describe his/her management style?

15. Can you describe his/her communication skills (both verbal and written)?

16. What do you think he/she could have done to produce even better results on the job?

17. If I were to ask other people he/she worked with, how do you think they would describe him/her on the job?

18. What do you think he/she needs to continue his/her own career development/professional growth?

19. What were his/her reasons for leaving? Why do you think he/she is looking for other employment opportunities? Could he/she have stayed if he'd/she'd wanted to?

20. If you were hiring people, would you hire him/her, and if you would, what do you think the ideal job would be for him/her?

21. Are you aware of any personal problems that could interfere with his/her ability to do the job for a prospective employer?

22. Is there anything else you'd like to add that we haven't talked about?

## SAMPLE QUESTIONS FOR LANDLORDS

1. How are you acquainted with (*name of prospective tenant*)?

2. How long did he/she rent from you?

3. What type of renter was he/she?

4. What was his/her payment history like?

5. Did you have any problems with him/her?

6. How did he/she get along with other tenants/renters?

7. What was the condition of the property when he/she left?

8. Would you rent to him/her again?

# From Barada Associates, Inc.

## SAMPLE REFERENCE REPORT

130 East Second Street • Rushville, Indiana 46173 • 765/932-5917 • Fax: 765/932-2938
E-mail: assignments@baradainc.com • Visit us at: http://www.baradainc.com

COMPANY NAME:

CANDIDATE:       JOHN SMITH
POSITION:        PRESIDENT

*Note: This sample reference report illustrates not only how much information can be obtained through careful reference checking, but also illustrates the point that frequently the reference will provide the information needed, but not necessarily in the order in which the questions would ordinarily be asked. It is a real reference report with only names and numbers changed. As you can see, this report covers a broad spectrum of job-performance-related topics that are carefully reviewed by a prospective employer to ensure that a candidate's overall job performance fits the requirements of the job to be filled. Particular concerns employers may have, either about the candidate or the special requirements of the position, can be easily integrated into the interview process.*

## FIRST REFERENCE

CONTACT:         BENSEN MILLER
                 SELF-EMPLOYED CONSULTANT
                 CARSON, VA
                 000/000-0000 (RESIDENCE)

RELATIONSHIP:    FORMER SUBORDINATE/ROSS/
                 MIDLAND/FLUORESCENT BALLAST,
                 INC.

"I have worked with John off and on approximately 15 years. We initially joined forces at Ross where John functioned as Vice President of Operations. Our division was located on Long Island in New York. We produced outdoor electrical lighting products in addition to servicing contracts. I later followed John to Midland Corporation, headquartered in Connecticut. John was Vice President and General Manager for a facility in South Bend, Indiana, and he oversaw a seven-plant operation. At that time, I functioned as Manager for Production Control and Director of Purchasing. The company made wires for automotive products. In 1992, John accepted a position as Vice President and General Manager with Fluorescent Ballast, Inc. in Virginia. This was a start-up effort, and John called me to join his organization. He basically started from nothing. The company produced fluorescent ballast and employed 200 people. I did all the logistics and supply and production control."

Specifically questioned about John's responsibilities at various organizations over the years, Bensen replied, "Above all, John is a pusher and knows how to get things done. With Midland, he turned the division around in a short time. For Fluorescent, he stepped up to the challenge and got the production line running in a fast and efficient manner. John has high standards, and he has always been very good dealing with customers."

Bensen rated John's overall performance very good, noting that in all cases John established and implemented programs and procedures. Bensen said, "John is an engineer by trade and looks closely at production setups. He knows where changes have to be made in order to make the business more effective and productive." According to Bensen, some of the companies they were associated with were union plants. "With Midland and Fluorescent, John worked long and hard with employees in order to avoid a union takeover. He has always been very good working with the various levels of an organization, including union officials."

Over the years, John has had numerous direct reports. Bensen explained at Fluorescent, John oversaw the efforts of engineering, production management, materials, purchasing, and marketing and sales. Talking about John's supervisory style, Bensen said that he puts a business plan together and informs the team how it is going to be implemented. "If we needed help, he was always available. John liked to get involved in everything, and for the most part, was participative. He was always there to lend a helping hand."

John was described as a good problem solver who is highly results-oriented. "John is a master of finance and remains aware of deadlines. Again, you must remember, he is an engineer and wants to make sure everything is in place." Bensen addressed John's experience with start-up efforts. "At Fluorescent, he had to set up pilot runs and liability testing. He checked and re-checked the demand for the product in the marketplace. John follows through and expects others to do the same. He was always aware of everything that was going on, and if there was a need for him to get involved with something, he would." In terms of pressure, Bensen said John faces it head-on and does whatever is necessary to complete a job. "He is a manufacturing guy through and through, and I think he thrives on pressure."

Bensen did not have any issues with John's ability to communicate with others either verbally or in writing. Asked what John could have done to produce better results over the years, Bensen said, "I really do not think he missed important goals established by the owners of the companies. He is a goal-oriented individual who doesn't like to fail."

Determined, strong-willed, and outgoing were terms used to describe John's personality. "Although he is very determined, John will listen if there is a problem or a snag in production. He listens to his staff's suggestions, and he holds himself accountable for the final decision." Talking about strong points, Bensen admired the way John attacks problems. He said John does things in a logical manner. "I also value the way he deals with his direct reports and their staff. His door is always open, yet he expects his people to do their jobs.

He lets the management team know what has to be accomplished, and he expects them to follow through."

Asked about areas for improvement or development, Bensen said, "John has been working as Vice President and General Manager for several years. What it boils down to is that his methods really work."

Bensen placed John near the top of the list compared to other managers he has worked with over the years. John was considered a workaholic who truly enjoys manufacturing. "John is motivated by hard work. He knows that being diligent will bring about positive rewards." For professional growth, Bensen encouraged John to stay in manufacturing.

Discussing others' perceptions of John, Bensen said most people would describe him as a "hard taskmaster who has achieved results. Overall, most people enjoyed working with him. He knows how to positively drive his employees to accomplish results."

Asked about John's departure from Ross, Bensen said he left that company as well as Midland for better opportunities. "Fluorescent was sold a couple of times during his employment with the organization. Not too long ago, the company finally closed its doors. I am really not sure of the reason for that decision."

"Currently, John is working with Communication Systems Corporation as General Manager, I believe. I think there is a lot of travel required in the position, and John wants to cut back on that." Bensen was unaware of anything that would have a negative impact on John's ability to perform in the future. Asked if he would hire John, Bensen laughed and said, "I have worked with him for many, many years, and yes, I would hire him if I had a manufacturing facility.

"In terms of his ability to handle the responsibilities of President, I know he can do it. Manufacturing is what John knows. With regard to start-up efforts, John can quickly lay out a plant the way it should

REFERENCE CHECKING FOR EVERYONE

be done and make minor changes in the manufacturing process operation whenever necessary. He has always been very good at that. John has experience in start-up situations, and he is effective at putting teams together. John Smith is definitely a solid choice."

## SECOND REFERENCE

CONTACT:  JIM JOHNSON
RETIRED DIRECTOR OF
MANUFACTURING
ABC MANUFACTURING COMPANY
SUMMER, FL
888/888-8888

RELATIONSHIP:  FORMER SUPERVISOR/FORMER
COLLEAGUE

Jim and John worked together about 20 years during the 1970s and 1980s at ABC, the world's largest wiring device company. ABC is a privately held company with sales in excess of $1 billion. Jim noted one individual owns the company. "John and I worked primarily on Long Island, where the company headquarters is located. We were also involved with plants in New England, New York, North Carolina, Mexico, and California. John was the active player in the development of a ground floor circuit interrupter that is now part of the required electrical code in construction. When John was first hired, he came to work for me. As a matter of fact, I originally hired him and brought him on board as my personal consulting engineer. Later, he accepted the responsibilities of Vice President of Operations for Brooklyn and Manhattan, where we were first colleagues. John reported to me for close to four or five years."

Jim was most impressed with John's engineering skills, noting, "His major contribution was engineering cost savings and development of the ground floor circuit interrupter. In addition, he knew how to manage a very large group of employees." Questioned about John's performance, Jim laughed and said, "He could find a less expensive way to make a product and still not destroy the quality. On a 1 to 10 scale, I rate his quality of work a 10. He always came through on projects I assigned to him. He never covered up problems, and he always spoke the truth."

Multitasking and meeting deadlines were not problems for John, according to Jim. "He was really a good down-to-earth, shirt-sleeve engineer. John was an around-the-clock worker, and I don't recall any problems with his ability to deal with the day-to-day pressures of his position."

John was considered a strong motivator and effective team manager. "He was very well liked by his colleagues. He would initially show what he wanted done and then get out of the way to let others do it. His employees knew they had to perform, but they also knew they would be recognized for their achievements. He really knew how to get others to rally behind his thoughts and ideas." In terms of interpersonal skills, Jim described John as a very straightforward and honest communicator. "If your client wants a straight shooter who will get things done, John is their man. He did a great job with union leaders in New York and Rhode Island. ABC had other facilities that were nonunion, and John did fine in that capacity as well."

John's verbal and written communication skills received excellent reviews. Jim quickly noted John has always been able to get his point across one-on-one or in a large group setting. Jim could not think of anything John could have done to enhance his performance.

In a more personal vein, John was characterized as dynamic, strategic, and outgoing. His follow-up skills, productivity, and financial ability in the area of budgeting were noted as strong points. Focusing on areas for improvement or development, Jim replied, "When he was first brought on board, I spent quite a bit of time and effort polishing a stone! John was a diamond in the rough. He has worked on honing his management skills over the years."

Jim has directed and been associated with numerous manufacturing executives over the years and said, "In my career, John Smith is number one. John is internally motivated and hell-bent to succeed. He is a go-getter, and I think a lot of that has to do with his upbringing." Due to the time that has lapsed since their association, Jim was unable to provide any specific advice for John's professional growth.

Commenting on others' perceptions of John, Jim said, "For the most part, people would say he was diligent and honest. Of course, you will always have personality clashes, but typically, he is known as a straight shooter first and foremost." Jim indicated John left ABC because of a personality clash with one of the senior vice presidents. "John left on his own, and so did several others because of this one particular individual who always passed the buck. John has had a successful career since he left ABC, and I think it was a wise choice for him to go." If Jim were in business today, he would hire John again. "The thing I really admired about John was the fact he always watched the store and made sure nothing went out the back door. He is definitely start-up material and has had plenty of experience in that arena. I would not be talking with you today if I did not think John Smith was an excellent choice for the position you have described."

## THIRD REFERENCE

CONTACT:        RICHARD BLACK
                      PRESIDENT
                      DEF CORPORATION
                      CRYSTAL LAKE, VIRGINIA
                      000/000-0000

RELATIONSHIP:     FORMER SUPERVISOR/FLUORESCENT
                  BALLAST CORPORATION

Richard hired John in January 1992 to begin a start-up division for one of his holding companies, Fluorescent Ballast Corporation. "I started that particular business, using resources from several of my other successful divisions. John and I worked closely together for two years until I sold Fluorescent to another organization. He was my General Manager and oversaw the day-to-day operations of the manufacturing facility. We produced a high volume of printed circuit boards. John was involved with production planning, engineering, inventory control, and purchasing. To a lesser extent, he also had marketing and sales responsibilities. I left the company when it was purchased in 1994, and John remained with the new organization."

Further discussing John's contributions, Richard said, "I credit him for getting the facility started. I have been involved with several commercial lighting ventures, and they are not easy to get started. John took the bull by the horns and moved the business ahead. He hired the people and correctly staffed the plant. He also established excellent vendor relationships."

Specifically questioned about John's performance and productivity, Richard said, "I was pleased with his efforts, and I would hire him again for a similar job. He handled the pressure well. He had done a lot of start-ups before he came to me. He was highly recommended by an executive recruiting firm in New Jersey. John came to us with skills in many different facets of manufacturing." At one point in time, John directly oversaw the efforts of 60 managers and supervisors. Richard considered him a hands-on and participative manager who worked well in a nonunion environment. "I know he was involved with union plants before, but there were never any hints of the desire for union activity in my organization." Richard suggested John did a fine job communicating up and down the ladder. He rated John's written work very good, noting his verbal communication skills were more than adequate.

Regarding presentation style, Richard said John appeared to be comfortable doing presentations to large groups. "He really was more comfortable when he knew his subject matter." Asked if there was anything John could have done to produce better results on the job, Richard replied, "I really do not think so. When I interviewed all the candidates for that position, I asked them to tell me about some of the mistakes or bad decisions they had made over the years. John remained in my mind as one of the most forthright candidates. He explained the things he had done wrong and how he had learned from his mistakes. He truly did his best for me, and his best was very good."

Richard described John as a very congenial guy who is conscientious and detail-oriented. "John is a doer and would be a rotten spectator. He is not one to stand on the sidelines and watch others. That is not to say he does the job for others, but he really enjoys getting involved." Discussing strong points, Richard said, "I was impressed with his ability to make something out of almost nothing. John is a great corporate chef! Give him the basic ingredients, and he will make the best stew possible. If your client has a business to start up, he will know what to do to get it going and keep things in perspective. That is what he does, and he does it very well. He will drive people hard, but he always recognizes their efforts."

With regard to areas for improvement, Richard could not think of anything specific. "If there were issues, John straightened things out immediately. He does whatever he can to take care of bad news."

John compared favorably to other general managers Richard has supervised and worked with. Accomplishing a task was identified as motivation for John. "He has always been keen on doing the best job he possibly can."

Richard believed others who have worked for or with John would describe him as "a fairly hard taskmaster." "John can be very demanding, but he expects no more of others than he expects of himself. I placed a lot of demands on him, and it was up to John to make sure orders were carried out. Usually the people who were upset were not as responsive or hardworking as they should have been. Overall, I really respected John for the driving and pushing he did." Richard said John left Fluorescent Ballast Corporation in 1996. "The company was sold a second time. I believe they just recently closed their doors."

Offering advice for John's professional growth, Richard said, "All people in management need to continue to hone their listening skills, including myself. We miss a lot because we do not listen as much as we should." Richard was unaware of anything that would have a negative impact on John's ability to perform in the future and highly recommended him for employment. "If John thinks he is qualified for the position, then he is. He will do his absolute best. He did for me."

## ACADEMIC INFORMATION

CONTACT: UNIVERSITY OF YOURTOWN
REGISTRAR'S OFFICE
YOURTOWN, CT
999/999-9999

CONFIRMED: John Smith, Social Security #000-00-0000, received a Master of Business Administration Degree on December 21, 1972.

## SUMMARY

References were quick to describe John Smith as a relatively hard taskmaster who drives himself as well as others to produce the best results possible. Over the past 25 years, John has been involved in all facets of manufacturing and has been successful in multi-operational management and start-up efforts. He is a true engineer at heart with an innate ability to find a way to manufacture a product in a less expensive manner and still not destroy its original quality. He is reliable and able to follow through, holding himself accountable for the end results. In the early 1990s, John was highly recommended to take on the start-up effort for Fluorescent Ballast Corporation. The former owner of the company had nothing but positive things to say about John's performance and overall effort. Subordinates and peers, as well as management, held John in high regard. In terms of his management style, he was described as participative, motivated, and results-oriented. He works and interfaces with others effectively both up and down the ladder. It was noted he maintained decent relationships with union officials.

In terms of his personality, John was characterized as down-to-earth, trustworthy, detail-oriented, and able to make things happen. References were hard-pressed to point to any concerns or deficiencies in his performance, noting when there was a problem or shortcoming, John took care of it. It seems John left his past employers for primarily the same reason, a better opportunity. He left Fluorescent in 1996 and has been working with Communication Systems since. According to references, John has the experience, know-how, and desire to implement procedures, and at the same time, rally his staff to keep things moving forward. At this point, John Smith appears to be a highly qualified candidate for President with your organization.

*Note: What else can be safely presumed from the comments contained in this report? Clearly, the candidate is a hard-driving individual who is results-oriented. Would he be a good candidate in a "caretaker" role as president of a company with a long-established tradition of doing things the same way? Definitely not. Would he be well suited for the presidency of a company with a more relaxed corporate culture? Again, definitely not. Is he going to potentially butt heads with equally hard-driving individuals? That seems very likely. Why? Based on what all three references said, the candidate has a solid history of outstanding performance in start-up situations and that he is hard-driving and a demanding taskmaster. Therefore, it is logical to assume that the strengths so consistently described could very well make him an unsuitable candidate for the types of situations just cited. As a hard-charger, in other words, it seems safe to assume that his style would not fit a caretaker role in a slow-paced environment. In addition, knowing that he is willing to butt heads with other hard-driving individuals would be very useful going into a relationship if, for no other reason, than to avoid any surprises down the road.*

*The point is that ensuring that the best hiring decision is made requires not only objectively evaluating the information contained in the report, but also weighing the information against both the realities of the job and the environment into which the candidate will have to function.*

# INDEX

# INDEX

# ABOUT THE AUTHORS

**Paul William Barada** is president and founder of Barada Associates, Inc., one of the few professional reference-checking services in the United States. Barada Associates' primary service is providing prospective employers with independent and objective assessments of past job performance on their candidates for employment. They currently serve companies from coast to coast, ranging from start-up businesses to the Fortune 100.

As a spokesman for reference checking in industry trade magazines and national media and, now, on the Internet, his articles have appeared in such publications as *Nation's Business, Human Resource Executive,* the *Employment Management Association Journal,* and *HR Magazine.* He has also been featured in *US News & World Report, Dun's Business Month, The New York Times, Time Magazine, Forbes, Industry Week, Indianapolis Monthly,* and *The Wall Street Journal.* He has served as The Reference Expert at Monster.com and currently serves as their Salary and Negotiations Expert.

Paul and his wife, Connie, have three sons: Paul Jr., Will, and Jonathan. They live in Rushville, Indiana.

Barada Associates, Inc. is located at:

130 East Second Street
Rushville, Indiana 46173
765/932-5917
E-mail: assignments@baradainc.com
www.baradainc.com

**J. Michael McLaughlin** is a South Carolina-based professional writer whose work has appeared in several national magazines. His travel guides and history readers are currently sold nationally. His freelance work as an advertising/marketing consultant has won national awards. He lives in Charleston.